CRISIS IN AMERICA:

FATHER ABSENCE

CRISIS IN AMERICA:

Father Absence

Frank Ancona

Nova Science Publishers Inc.
Commack, N.Y.

Assistant Vice President/Art Director: Maria Ester Hawrys
Office Manager: Annette Hellinger
Graphics: Frank Grucci and John T'Lustachowski
Acquisitions Editor: Tatiana Shohov
Book Production: Ludmila Kwartiroff, Christine Mathosian and Tammy Sauter
Editorial Production: Susan Boriotti
Circulation: Cathy DeGregory and Maryanne Schmidt

Library of Congress Cataloging-in-Publication Data

Ancona, Francesco Aristide. 1947-
Crisis In America: Father Absence / by Frank Ancona
      p.   cm.
     Includes bibliographical references (p. 132) and index.
     ISBN 1-56072-569-9
     1. Fathers -- United States. 2. Fatherless Families—United States. 3. Paternal Deprivation
–United States. 4. Social Problems—United States. 5. United States—Social Conditions—
1980- . I. Title.
HQ756.A57   1998   98-7503
306.874'2—dc21   CIP

Copyright © 1998 by Nova Science Publishers, Inc.
               6080 Jericho Turnpike, Suite 207
               Commack, New York 11725
               Tele. 516-499-3103   Fax 516-499-3146
               E-Mail: Novascience@earthlink.net
               Web Site: http://www.nexusworld.com/nova

Printed in the United States of America

To Fathers and my Father –

To Mothers and my Mother—

To son and daughters – all!

Do I contradict myself?
Very well then I contradict myself.
(I am large, I contain multitudes.)
Walt Whitman
from *Song of Myself*

AUTHOR'S PREFACE

I am a comparative mythologist, that is, I study the myths of peoples from all over the world and throughout time, from the prehistoric epoch to the present day – here and now. But "study" isn't really the right word. I enjoy them. I love them. I live them. To me, mythologies are as essential to our survival as the air we breathe and the food we eat, for they act as "clutches" between the feelings, ideals and fantasies contained within us and the concrete world we inhabit without. Just the way an automobile's clutch helps mesh the gears of its transmission to its engine, our mythologies "mesh" all the wonderment that is inside each of us human beings – our consciousness and unconsciousness, our rationality and creativity, our emotions, dreams, delusions, fears and aspirations – to the external world of our environment. In short, mythologies connect us, each of us as individuals, to the "all else" out there. So, to me, mythologies are forever present and eternally essential to our living the life we are fortunate enough to have inherited. And *living* is the key to it all. Mythologies are not about reflecting on life or discovering the meaning or even the "mystery" of life. Mythologies do not dissect life or subject it to any scientific method of understanding. Mythologies simply help us to *live* life. Life is to be *LIVED*, not contemplated. Consequently, the most important mythology is the one you are living right now. You are, this moment, living a mythology.

Without a mythology, you cease to live and begin, instead, to merely survive.

I am bringing all this up now for a reason. I am beginning to recognize a disturbing trend in America today: We are losing our mythologies. The once grandiose quality of life in America with its eternal wellspring of hope is rapidly giving way to a grossly diminished way of life, the mere survival of everyday atrocities. What was once unthinkable as accepted behavior in America – child molestation, capricious destruction of life and property, the veneration and romanticizing of the substance addicted and criminally deviant, the killing of newborn infants in public rest rooms by their own mothers, partial birth abortions – is now the evening news, every evening, seven days a week, all year-round.

As a result, the "darlings" of rock, rap, Hollywood and the sports arena are now worshipped mostly for their denigrating and disgusting behavior. Celebrity is, today, deviance. You see, the positive mythopoeic process in America is, in fact, all but lost. And, tragically, it is being replaced by a destructive system of purposeful propaganda. Thus, instead of liberating mythologies, we have controlling messages. Let me explain. Myths are the products of individuals – artists, shamans, visionaries, pioneers – whatever you would like to call them. Mythologies have always been the work of individuals: Jesus and Buddha., Mohammed, Black Elk, and Martin Luther King, Einstein and Edison, Copernicus, Goethe and Van Gogh. Their mythologies, their "dreams," are accepted and embraced by the masses, but they did not originate with the "people." They began with the individual and were later adopted by the "folk." Every society needs these individuals, these "heroes" and, of course, just as importantly, its "heroines" – Joan of Arc, Mary Cassals, Queen Elizabeth, Golda Meir, Mother Teresa, Margaret Thatcher, Madame Curie – as well. The emphasis, though, is always on the "individual." Ironically, this rugged individuality has always been America's strongest point, its greatest mythology. The mythology we call the "American Dream" was built on the strength of the individualism of our citizenry, on our individual freedom. Until now, that is.

Now, everything has changed. The emphasis is on the "group" and on "normalizing" society and "fitting in." Ours is a nation of hyphenated "gangs" struggling for power, so that members of "in" gangs are awarded preferential treatment over those unfortunate enough to be trapped in "out" gangs. We are "this"-American and "that"-American, so much so the very concept of individual freedom is under attack. So is free speech. Someday you won't even have a voice. And it doesn't stop there. Our political system is in danger. Our two-party system is about to dissolve. Worse, we are told to seek political bipartisanism, that those with different points of view should find a common "middle ground." We are taught that any judgment of one another is wrong, that all is "relative" and, therefore, by extension, "acceptable." Authority figures – police, teachers, parents, corporate leaders, even our ancestors – have been recast as oppressive and hypocritical villains, to the point that now the rights of criminals are equal to the rights of their victims. Criminals aren't the problem in bad neighborhoods, we are told; the police are the problem. Police brutality is the real danger.

Today, our children are brainwashed, discouraged from competitive ventures, by social engineers who have turned our education system into a holding pen to (as Shakespeare would have phrased it) "suckle fools" by stroking their self-esteem and rewarding them for not trying and, therefore, not failing. For, think about it, how can you fail if you don't try? Watch any television situation comedy; you'll see children projected as knowing as much as, if not more than, their parents. The rebellious behavior and snide wisecracking of these idolized youths is an affront to any parent trying hard to instill values and morality in his or her child. Perhaps, worst of all, you'll see children who study hard and maintain civility portrayed as "nerds," ridiculed and scorned as misfits.

It's obvious, isn't it: There is a systematic, concentrated effort to replace the structuring mythology of America, the "American Dream," of rugged individualism and competition with a weak process of socialization, a failed third-world model. Our schools and institutions of higher education are bastions of liberalism where, ironically, socialism – though it is losing ground to democracy all over the world – still thrives. There's a joke that, when Russia fell, the socialists asked what are we going to do with all these socialistic tracts and treatises and were told, sell them to America's colleges and universities. There's a lot of truth in that, for this same socialistic perspective permeates our media, our political system, our sports arenas, our music, and Hollywood – which, to me, is the most hypocritical occurrence one can imagine: All the big media, political, music, sports, and Hollywood "stars," though they preach extreme versions of liberalism to us, live like aristocracy in mansions and "compounds," isolated and protected from the "rabble" like French royalty before the French revolution. Everyday, I see "bleeding hearts" imploring us to be more concerned – worse, scolding us for not giving or doing enough – for the "lowest of the low," who they drag out like salespeople drag out displays. Then I see them photographed, these "feel good about themselves" humanitarians in their secluded paradises, living the elitist "lifestyles" of the rich and famous.

Imagine if one of us "everyday people" should show up! Not only would they have us carted away, but also they would disinfect the areas we profaned by our presence. In fact, they would probably have to go hunt out a whole new paradise even further away from us.

Yet we don't see through the "sham" and hypocrisy. We allow them to sell us on socialism while they live in a separate realm of celebrity. If anything is causing polarization in America, it is not capitalism. The liberal and wealthy "elite" are moving further and further from the masses. This is why we have got to wake up to the truth because this forced and artificial "norming" is leading to America's destruction, for ours is a country built on the principle of "equal opportunity," not equal results. Equality is not a goal; it is a starting point. The same lifestyle the "limousine" liberal elite want for themselves is exactly the lifestyle they should want for us. The mythology that once structured America called for an equal playing field, not that every game end in a tie score. But the great individualists who gave birth to America are gone now, so are their mythologies. Their heroic individualism has been replaced by politically correct "gangs," who dictate what we think and how we should respond. "Once upon a time," there was free speech in America. Now, Americans are punished for what they say – even when their words happen to be overheard in private conversations – and, if not imprisoned, chastised or removed from their career positions, they are sent to endure the banality of "sensitivity" training, conducted by rigid-minded robots, who are themselves, ironically, insensitive to any other point of view or expression of perspective and who are busily "milking" the system for their own monetary and career self gain. How far away from "gulags" are we? It is not coincidental that such horrid political penal institutions came from a government – an "evil empire" – that systematically and purposefully suppressed its spirituality and mythologies, replacing them with the "unity" of a single-voiced media. And it's not coincidental that we are now moving in the same direction.

And what is their power over us? They have no power other than what we cede by joining or enduring them. The only power they have is the power we give them. So why do we give them any? Ours is an America of sheep, an America of "cowed" followers, who seek only the protection of the herd, even if the herd has no effective leadership and is governed by "bull shitters" instead of bulls. In fact, we are no longer really comfortable with powerful leaders. We like our leaders to be one of us, to "feel our pain," and, more importantly, to never separate us from the flock, so we are never ever left behind – heaven forbid – to fend for ourselves, on our own – free and responsible. Today's leaders talk of "building a bridge" to the

21st century as if the turn of the millennium is some sort of magical moment that we must be prepared to confront. The real danger is their self-aggrandizement. Niccolo Machiavelli's advice to his prince was, roughly, to tell the people a great danger was just outside the door (or, in our case, at the turn of a century) and that you, their leader, was all the defense they had to protect them. And, as Machiavelli sagaciously concluded, the people would blindly follow you forever. With all due respect to those anticipating the apocalypse of the 21st century, there is no more "magic" in the turn of the millennium as there is in the turn from any one moment to the next on any given day. Image over substance – that's the leadership we have today: Leadership that serves itself by creating a fear in the people to control them. What disdain for "we, the people"! Yet it is our fault, for we have become cowards. The intrepid souls who built this once free nation didn't wait for a bridge to be built or a new millennium to spark them to action; rather, they carved this great country out of the wilderness, braving danger and suffering personal injury. These "pioneers" weren't apathetic, or did they wait for someone else to do it. Believe it or not, they did everything for themselves. After all, this was once the "land of the brave." Or have we forgotten? Or, worse, can't we tell anymore because of our current craven state?

You see, our American spirit of adventure is gone. The mythology of the American pioneer is dead. We've lost it. We've lost our "American dream." We are not a country of immigrants, as people erroneously conclude. We are a country of pioneers, and those pioneers came here with their dreams and the desire to build an America. They wanted to be in a land where their hard work and vision would be rewarded. They wanted to live in a free country, where their differences would be accepted. Those who came in later waves also wanted to become Americans, not hyphenated Americans. Their ethnic backgrounds and points of origin did not come first before the word American. They were Irish and Italian and Black and Spanish and Oriental and every race imaginable, yet they all shared one dream, to *become* American. Their goal was to become proud Americans, not to try and make Americans ashamed of themselves. They did not come here to replace the American culture with their own while, ironically, living off the people they sought to usurp. Let us be clear here, no true American is against legal immigration. What every American is against are those who come to this country and, tragically, hate it and seek to destroy it. Such hatred should not go unopposed! Yet it is. In fact, we are castigated for even thinking about fighting back against those who declare war on us. Why? The answer is simple. We have no heroes to lead us. The pioneer spirit has been replaced by a lazy indifference, an apathy, centered around the selfish desire to be left alone. The myth of adventure is gone. The very idea of fighting back, let alone fighting, is hated. We are emasculated. We are being "conditioned" to not make trouble. So we endure the bullying of self-interested radicals, more and more each and every day in the mistaken belief that – eventually – when they get what they want, they will stop. Well, appeasement never works. They don't stop, not ever, not as long as they know they can push us around.

Today, nearly all Americans are living vicariously. It's almost as if we've lost the stomach for risk and the heart for adventure. Instead, we live through public figures, entertainers and athletes – the more outlandish and insane the better, for celebrity is worshiped in and of itself, so much so, it does not matter how it is obtained. Thus, even our celebrities are different now; they are no longer heroes or heroines who earned their tributes. They are simply in the spotlight. We seek their visibility. We are attracted to them, not for what they have achieved. Think about it: Most of them *did* absolutely nothing!

They are celebrities simply because they are illuminated wherever they go, accompanied by music, banners, and waving crowds. We have political leaders who don't lead; rather, they hire statistical analysts and image consultants then simply follow the polls and public opinion. We have entertainers who are anything but entertaining. We have actors who cannot act let alone conduct themselves civilly or maturely yet who believe themselves to be political pundits, preaching one lifestyle for us while they live another behind electrical fences in mansions and guarded compounds. They surround themselves with bodyguards and travel in circles that disdain any contact with the "great unwashed." We have six foot tall, eighty-five pound "super" models who starve themselves and "peak" career-wise at about fifteen. And why are they "super"? Did they do something? No, they simply pose. Ah, image in America has certainly supplanted substance, hasn't it? Lastly, let us not forget our athletes, who sign multi-million dollar contracts while they are still in school – notice, I didn't call them students because "study" often has very little to do with the time they spend at college – and are more interested in hits of cocaine than those listed in the box scores, more famous for the scoring they do off the field than for their performance in the game. By the way, just ask one of these guys to be a role model. You know what you'll hear? "That's not my job." And, you know, for once, I find myself agreeing with them.

Even the highest office in our land is subject to this hollow concept of celebrity. Our presidency, today, is not defined in terms of leadership.

Contemporary presidents don't actually have to *do* anything anymore; our presidents just have to be enthroned or, better yet, be social lions. Our presidency is defined in terms of "listenership." Polls rule despite the admonition we know to be so painfully true, "Figures don't lie but liars figure." Consequently, our presidents no longer need to lead; they simply need to follow from "in front." Sadly, our concept of an "ideal" president is a "communicator," more comfortable in the spotlight and in front of microphones than on the front lines – image over substance.

It took an artist to intuit the truth and warn us, but we didn't understand then what Andy Warhol meant by our "fifteen minutes of fame," and we don't understand now. When people feel the invisibility of the herd, all that matters is getting into the limelight, no matter how. So a mass murderer is cheered. A gang "hit man" is a celebrity. A corrupt politician signs autographs and writes books for multi-million dollar advances. False accusers are rewarded with million dollar "out-of-court" settlements. And prostitutes of all kinds make guest appearances on late night television – selling, selling, selling the public the latest garbage "fad" – while all day long on the same medium people, egged on by jeering crowds, deface and denigrate themselves, their families, and their loved ones by confessing to any and every depravity just to get on camera.

But what's worse is we *watch*! We watch and watch and watch – the more gruesome, the better. And whatever is there we accept. We are told how to think and what to think. Everything we see and hear has a "spin" on it. We have no news media. Nearly 90% of "reporters" vote democratic in every election – imagine how many are socialists – so we have no objectivity in their reporting; rather, every major network covers stories the exact same way at the same time, in "lockstep," like the reporting arm of a dictator's third world operation. They have even usurped the "voice of the people." We are *told* the results of polls. We are *told* what the "people" think. But all of it is a fraud. What we're actually being told is what the media think. They dictate what the people believe. They tell us what we believe and what to believe, and it all becomes a self-fulfilling prophesy: After they tell us what we believe, we believe it – then they report that we believe it. What a vicious cycle! There isn't a "double standard"; there's no standard. Our once great "news" profession has managed to denigrate itself so much newspeople are now held in less esteem than lawyers and politicians. And, ironically, the organs of the media once ridiculed as inferior – radio and weekly "scandal rags" – are the only ones breaking stories, unless you count foreign newspapers. Instead of "radio free Europe," we'll soon need a "radio free America" – news coming from abroad to get the truth. Is it no wonder "talk" radio is growing in popularity? Where else can Americans speak their minds? Where else can an honest argument be aired? That's why it's so feared, why it's labelled as "hate radio" by those who hate it for being "free and open." Look what's happened: Our media has entrapped us behind an iron curtain; like the old "evil empire," we need to turn to underground and foreign sources to get the truth. Even more tragically, we are told that what we have seen with our own eyes, what we have heard with our own ears, we didn't really see or hear. Our history, itself, has been rewritten. Even the immediate past that we lived ourselves has been changed, rescripted – and we accept the new scenario despite the fact we know it's a lie. Why? Because everything is being done for "our own good." *They* know what's right for us. And they'll get it done even if it hurts. Why? Because their "ends justify the means," *any* means – lies, distortions are fine. And, when the messages are too difficult to dispel or distort, the messengers are attacked and portrayed as "vile" and "vicious" – "mean spirited" and against the good that's trying to be done. You see, for gangs to rule, there must be no opposition, no individualism. If anyone dares to disagree, that person is marginalized, denigrated and labeled: "racist," "homophobe," "chauvinist," "Uncle Tom." Pick one, the label doesn't really matter; it exists only to humiliate, like the scarlet letter Hester Prynne was forced to wear. It doesn't matter whether you display an "A" on your breast, the mark of Cain on your forehead, or the label of racist or chauvinist. What matters is that you are silenced and ostracized for breaking silence and getting in the way. Think about it, for the most part, what we used to know as "free speech" in America is now considered "hate mongering." If someone does not agree with the "politically correct," that person is now considered evil. A different opinion is now illegal. What ever happened to the idea that, even if I disagree with what you say, I will fight to the death for your right to say it"? Another dead mythology, "rolling over in its grave."

The worst part of America's current dilemma is that no one has the courage to oppose the purposeful dissolution of our country. It's almost as if all the greatness of America – our forging of freedom, our vast lauding of the individual, our liberating heroism in world wars – never happened, wasn't real. Instead, we have been conditioned to act like America is something to be *ashamed* of. We are constantly *apologizing*, seeking to make reparations. We apologize profusely – or, rather, our President apologizes on our behalf – for our unfortunate flaws and ignore the vast majesty of our unparalleled accomplishments. How tragically ironical is it that America is called an oppressor by dictators! The portrayal of this still magnificent nation as a vile and selfish bastion of evil capitalism and human rights abuses is a lie, a damned lie! Ours is and has always been – from its conception – the greatest nation on the face of the earth! Yet so few of us even feel comfortable defending ourselves anymore, let alone going on the offense, fighting for what we believe. So few of us have the courage to stand up and shout, "The emperor has no clothes," for we have so few heroes, so few "individual" voices to oppose the ever spreading cancer of mob rule and anti-American propaganda. The brave voices of heroes, mythologies – for that's what mythologies are, the brave voices of heroes – are rapidly becoming figments of a "once upon a time" in America.

So how did this happen to us? When did we lose our American dream? Where is our heroic "individualism" and the mythologies it envisions? How did we go from the greatest nation on earth to truly "third world" status? When did our glorious country deteriorate? Why are we afraid to walk down the streets of our cities? Why can't we visit our parks, our museums, our galleries? Why is drug use – why are all dependencies, like those on "big government" – accepted, even glorified in mass media, "tinsel town," and rock videos when we know their horrors? In fact, why are so many of our people so *dependent*? Why is the fabric of our society unravelling? When did our youth get so out of control? When did we lose them? Why do we have such a growing welfare state? Who destroyed our education system? Our children can't read, can't write, can't add, know nothing of science or of our *true* history, yet we reward them and assure them they are "all right." Why aren't we upset over this? Not only do we accept their ignorance, but also we encourage it; we tell them whatever they do is fine because we are a people who make no judgments. We don't criticize. We don't dare traumatize. We accept, accept, accept – anything and everything. We accept blame. We accept hatred. And we accept the decline of our once great nation.

Is this because we just don't care? But, if we just don't care, then why does all this hurt so much? Why are fire fighters and police villainized and hindered from doing their jobs? Why do people throw rocks and debris at fire fighters as these brave heroes try to put out fires in these people's very own neighborhoods? Why are the police perceived to be "evil" and not the drug dealers, rapists, and murderers? Why are our children having children? Why are we becoming so racially polarized? Why are criminals set free by juries of their peers simply because of their color? Why are drug dealers and violent offenders accepted in, and protected by, their neighborhoods? What have they done for their people? What have they done for America? And when did men and women come to *hate* each other?

America is coming apart at the seams! Why do children have to be fingerprinted? Why are rape statistics skyrocketing? How many pedophiles are there that we must endure the broadcasting of their loathsome carnage night after night, their gruesome rapes and murders of our defenseless children televised into our homes each and every evening. All the rapists! All the murderers! Why? Why do we endure this "outrageous fortune"? Why isn't it "nobler in our minds" to "take arms against a sea of troubles," and "by opposing end it"! What does it say about us, America, when mindless rock stars, B-actors, and teenage athletes have millions of dollars thrown at them to squander on gold chains and earrings, pills, powders to snort, and sports cars to roll over while millions of our neglected, forgotten, and – sadly – unwanted children go to bed hungry or are dumped in a trashcan the minute they're born? What does it say about America when we label a whole generation of children with the heartbreaking letter "X"? It says we are a disgrace!

I believe it was the preeminent historians Will and Ariel Durant who once observed something to the effect that given the choice between freedom and order, people will choose order. Why isn't this true anymore in contemporary America? It used to be. Americans once fought for what they believed. Americans once sacrificed their selfish desires for the good of our people because they knew that, ironically, out of order came freedom. Isn't that what our late President John F. Kennedy meant when he admonished, "Ask not what your country can do for you. Ask what you can do for your country." What's happened to that maturity of vision? What's happened to Martin Luther King's "dream"? Where is the leader who will call upon us to raise arms against these "days of infamy"? Where is our Mandela to encourage and inspire us to embrace the "light" over the darkness? Gone. We lost everything – we lost it all – when we lost our central, structuring mythology: *patriarchy*.

Now, we are *without fathers*. We are without the paternal function that is responsible for maturing individuals and weaning them away from the selfish dependencies of adolescence. We have emasculated our nation. Today, in America, all things masculine are evil. Everything male is to be opposed and rejected, replaced by a "new and better" feminine sensitivity that accepts all things as equal in its unconditional generosity and desire for total inclusion – even of our criminals, our rapists, and murderers. The only problem is, in our desire to accept equally everyone and everything, we cheapen it all, so it is no longer special and, thus, not really worth having. In Kurt Vonnegut's delightful, comedic "fabulation" – partly myth, partly novel – about the nature of paternity played out in the economic realm, *God Bless You, Mr. Rosewater*, patriarch Senator Lister Ames Rosewater castigates his philanthropist son Eliot for his unrestricted "giving": "You're the man who stands on a street corner with a roll of toilet paper, and written on each square are the words, 'I love you.' And each passerby, no matter who, gets a square all his or her own. I don't want my square of toilet paper" (90). From the Senator's perspective, such unrestricted giving is not only destructive, but also self-serving. Consequently, whether or not we agree with Lister Ames Rosewater is not important; what is important is the paternal voice and direction he provides. For fathers *are* important. Fathers teach us about restrictive love, about the value of love when it is earned instead of thrown at us. Fathers bring us to maturity. Fathers help us achieve independence. Fathers provide us with identities. Fathers encourage us to "push the envelope" and take risks. They make us strive to become better and better. We *need* our fathers!

Once upon a time, America was the greatest nation on the face of the earth. Once upon a time, there were fathers in America.

Acknowledgements

Many thanks and much love goes to my wife Janet, who loves me and believes in me completely, even in those moments when I don't believe in myself. Thanks and love also, to my sister JoAnn, whose admiration and support have always kept me going.

Thanks, always, to the memory of my beloved parents, whose love animates my soul. And thanks to the late Dr. Edward Guereschi, whose memory I will always cherish and to whom I am deeply indebted for guidance, wisdom, and "good-hearted perspicuity".

Thank you to all my friends and relatives, colleagues and students-- you make up my world, and more importantly, make it beautiful.

Our deepest fear is not that we are inadequate. Our deepest fear is that we are powerful beyond measure. It is our light, not our darkness, that most frightens us. We ask ourselves, who am I to be brilliant, gorgeous, talented and fabulous? Actually, who are you not to be? You are a child of God. Your playing small doesn't serve the world. There is nothing enlightened about shrinking so that other people won't feel insecure around you. We are born to make manifest the glory of God that is within us. It's not just in some of us; it's in everyone. And as we let our own light shine, we unconsciously give other people permission to do the same. As we are liberated from our own fear, our presence automatically liberates others.

"Our Deepest Fear", Marianne Williamson
From *A Return to Love.*

Violence – senseless violence. Gangs. Rape. Crime. Murder. Substance abuse. Denigration of women. Racism. No conscience. No remorse. Reckless promiscuity. Irresponsibility. Divorce and single-parenting. Babies having babies. Abortion as birth control. Dependence on government as a way of life. Rebellion. Hatred of authority and authority figures. An educational system in crisis. Victim mentality. The loss of religion and spirituality. Polarization. What am I describing here? Unfortunately, the behaviors and attitudes of an ever growing segment of our American youth. Why? How did this happen? Many blame the dissolution of the family. But that's incorrect. The dissolution of the family is, most certainly, a tragedy; however, it is merely a symptom, not a cause.

The cause is the loss of the paternal function. In short, we are without fathers.

But what is a father? What is the paternal function? Why do we need fathers? How did we lose our fathers? And, most importantly, how can we get them back and get back, too, America the way it "used to be"?

"You're a fool if you follow the rules," is, unfortunately, only one of America's vast new breed of destructive mythologies that are, tragically, replacing those once proud and effective patriarchal mythologies born out of America's individualistic quest for its "dream."

But – wait – how can there be "new" mythologies? Aren't mythologies the crusty old stories of ancient peoples in long ago forgotten parts of the world? Of course not, and they never were. Mythologies are not fantastical, "dead" stories with little to no meaning for us today; rather, what we perceive as the whimsical and useless tales of "primitive" peoples are, in truth, extremely valuable utilitarian structures, around which human lives and societies throughout time and space have been constructed. They needed their mythologies then as we need ours now: to survive. Consequently, the mythopoeic process is a "living," essential element of being human. Therefore, new mythologies are being created all the time, so the creation of new mythologies is not the problem. The problem for contemporary America is the destructive nature and origin of its "new" mythologies. Succinctly, the mythologies of America have changed; unfortunately, they have not changed for the better.

So who is creating these destructive mythologies? And why?

Mythologies come from individuals. They are then embraced by the masses, who ultimately adopt them as their own, but they are first and foremost created by individuals – "visionaries." Therefore, our answer cannot simply be that, "America is always evolving; consequently, its mythologies are constantly changing." Anyway, that philosophy only provides us with a possible explanation of change itself; it cannot give us any reason for the specific, negative changes America is currently experiencing. No, we cannot say the unfortunate and tragic changes we perceive in contemporary America are products of a long, slow process of a "natural" cultural evolution. They are not! This is not to say that the undermining of America has not been moving incrementally over the last half century. It has been, but not as a process of "natural" evolution. The destruction of America by infiltrating its very structure and perverting it, turning it against itself, has been a well-planned, purposeful process. Our education system has been invaded and defeated. Our political system has been invaded and defeated. Our judicial system has been invaded and defeated. Our media has been invaded and defeated. Our entertainment industry has been invaded and defeated. Slowly – purposefully – little by little in such small, hardly noticeable steps, the cancered areas progress and aren't even recognized until they literally outnumber the healthy cells, making them almost impossible to remove – so much so that today, the once powerful "silent majority" no longer exists; tragically, its own silence has silenced it, so – yes – it is still silent, but it is no longer a majority. Ironically, however, despite the insidious incubation period, the horrors of America today have really come about relatively quickly and from identifiable sources.

Yet, before we explore this apparent incongruity, allow me to return briefly to the opening line of this section, "You're a fool if you follow the rules." Perhaps, this will lead us in the right direction, especially if we ask ourselves how this disreputable philosophy gained credence in contemporary America. How *did* such a lawless mythology of "do unto others before they do unto you" replace the "golden rule" of doing unto others as we would wish others to do unto us? Do you even believe me now when I tell you it has? "You're a fool if you follow the rules," is so repugnant to most of us we do not even believe it has become part of America's mythology. Nevertheless, despite this incredulity, it has. And it has permeated every layer of society from the highest office in the land, the President of the United States, to our school children. Here's an example: Recently there was a news story about two New York high schools that were suffering through such a severe rivalry all basketball games between them had to be canceled because, inevitably, the games would result in violence. But that wasn't the news. The news was that school officials from both high schools got together to "try again"; the two teams would, once again, face each other on the basketball court. Well, the result was no surprise: Violence erupted!

And, as expected, the local news media flocked to the event. One reporter shoved a microphone in the face of some young boys who had obviously been fighting and asked, "What's wrong with you kids, today? Don't you know right from wrong?" I hope when you hear their answer it shocks you, for, if it doesn't, then truly we have no hope. One of the boys spoke for the group, "Sure, we know right from wrong," he boasted, his face beaming with an ear-to-ear grin, "but no one's ever told us which is better!"

"No one's ever told us which is better" – with all due apologies to Shakespeare, there's the "rub"! *Who* should have told them? Whose voice is missing? Who is responsible for "laying down the law"? The answer is simple: the Father. Fathers are the "guarantors" of the "law." They are responsible for setting and enforcing the rules. It is the father's function to teach his children *why* right is better than wrong, *why* it is better to live by the "golden rule" than the mistaken notion you're a fool if you follow the rules. The absence of the father in America is the reason this once great nation, the mightiest nation on the face of the earth, is now rapidly deteriorating into third world status. America has lost its patriarchal structure and guidance. Contemporary America is a nation without discipline. We do not know which is better, right or wrong. This is why our President and our media in his defense can use the excuse, "Everybody does it," when caught with the proverbial hand in the cookie jar. I don't know about everyone else, but I'm sick of that defense! I don't do it, and – even if I did – that wouldn't make it right. If everyone went around stabbing everyone else, would that make stabbing each other permissible? They know what is right and what is wrong; they are just confused, and trying to confuse us, about which is better.

You see, we are without fathers. Consequently, there is no one with the courage to stand up and say, "I don't care if 'everybody does it.' This is the law. This is what's right, and this is what's wrong."

Here's the problem: We are mired in a state of "relativism," that is, nothing is perceived as right or wrong; instead, everything is debatable, arguable and, worse, embraced. Everything, no matter what it is, no matter how deviant, insane, or destructive, must be accepted for fear of excluding or offending. The idea seems to be we must accept everything or nothing, for if we refuse to condone one tiny bit all will be lost. But, as we all know, this "relativism" is wrong! Time, as Einstein demonstrated, may be relative, but our times ought not to be. Yet the question of equity remains: Is it *fair* to be conditional? And, if we are conditional, do we lose the concept of equality? Here, mythology proves most valuable, for one of the first epiphanies of mythology is the revelation that, ultimately, all opposites prove to be the same. What does this mythological "epiphany" mean? It means that we can be conditional without losing our sense of fairness and inclusion. In fact, it means we must be conditional in order to become unconditional, and if we insist on being unconditional we become, ironically, conditional. Isn't this the truth in America today where "political correctness" has itself become more demagogical than the insensitivity it sought to usurp? How many instances can you recall where political correctness has resulted in the stifling of free speech rather than in its preservation? How many people have been hurt by political correctness? You know the answer: An awful lot – because this irony is a part of our everyday lives. I realize this may not make a great deal of sense and is open to an even greater deal of criticism, but this is exactly the point: Mythologies speak to us from another source deeper than reason. They *don't* make sense. They are *not* to be understood. We just "feel" they are correct even though we cannot understand why. Consequently, we cannot explain why relativism leads to its opposite, or why a society that enforces strict laws may create, ironically, an atmosphere of great freedom. We just know – not in our minds – in our hearts. Here's a quick example: A society that does not give equal rights to its criminal class, that, instead, reveres and respects its law enforcement and judicial systems, provides a safe environment for its law-abiding citizenry while, conversely, a society "humane" in its attitudes towards those poor, "misguided individuals" who rob, maim, rape, and murder, creates an environment of fear not freedom. For what is more humane – to care about the humane citizenry or to care about *all* the citizens regardless of their lack of humanity? You know the answer. To forgive the unforgivable, is itself, unforgivable! You know it in your heart.

Thus, we can lay down rules – even absolutes – without destroying the entire concept of civil and individual liberties. In fact, the society which lacks the courage to "lay down the law" is the one that will lose its freedom and hurt its people. Let's take the AIDS epidemic, for example. If our leaders only had the courage in the beginning to stand up to the radical group of "advocates" who demanded AIDS be turned into a political rather than an epidemiological issue, how many tens of thousands of lives would have been saved? How many hundreds of thousands? When the first cases in America presented themselves (I believe in Long Island), if we had the courage then to follow the laws we use for every other type of possible epidemic and quarantined those first cases, how different would things be now? How many young people would be alive and well right now? We lacked the guts then to proceed the way we knew we should have – not in any prejudiced way, in the exact same way we would deal with *any* other health threat – and we lack the guts now to even blame those "activists" more interested in political and personal gain than human life – or to even blame ourselves for our loss of courage and common sense. I'd love to know, is it me? Am I crazy? Or do others believe human lives are more important than humane issues?

I don't care if you're "gay" or "straight." That's not the issue. The issue is, if we could have quarantined some individuals then – in compliance with the law – and, admittedly, have denied them of some rights in the process, but that action resulted in the saving of your life, or your lover's life and the lives of countless other wonderful and valuable people, what would you have done? Are the loss of some civil rights more valuable than the loss of lives? I guess they are when "ideals" are valued over persons. I'd rather hurt the feelings of a few than sacrifice the lives of hundreds of thousands of people to a "principle" not worth the poster its printed on, you know, the one the "advocates" are forever flaunting in our faces, thanks to the ever-accommodating media. No, let's not be afraid to hurt someone if the pain is for his or her own good. Remember this voice: "Better you cry now a little bit than I cry a lot for you later." That's a parent's voice. That's a father's voice. That's the voice of someone not afraid to set laws or to enforce them. But where is that voice? Where are our fathers?

III

What is a father? What is the paternal function? Why do we need fathers? How did we lose our fathers? And, most importantly, how can we get them back?

Succinctly, a father is responsible for, and essential to, the maturation processes of his children, be they males or females. Ironically, like the mother, the father also gives "birth." Just as the gestating embryo matures in the mother's womb before it is physically born from her, the birthed child matures in the symbolical womb of the father – to be born, metaphorically, a "second time" from him. The mother's egg is a nurturing and protective shell. So too is the father. Figuratively speaking, he too is an "egg" who protects and nurtures his children. Upon their maturation, his children are born from him symbolically just as they were born physically from their mother. Thus, the function of this paternal "egg" is to provide the physical security and nourishment his children need to gain psychic independence and achieve individual and societal identities. It is, therefore, the father's primary function to bring his birthed children – sons and daughters, alike – to maturity.

Today, America's children are suffering, in ever greater and greater numbers, from this catastrophic loss of the paternal function. But this tragic state of affairs is only the proverbial "tip of the iceberg." As detrimental as father loss is for the maturation process of individual children, it is far more deleterious for the maturation process of the country itself. Let me explain. Most observers correctly recognize the loss of the paternal function as a "root" cause of the dissolution of the family in contemporary America. And fatherless children are most definitely the cause, in turn, of many societal woes, which this book – rightly so and in good time – will attempt to address in depth. However, the impact of father absence goes far beyond this family perniciousness. The loss of the paternal function has undermined the very social fabric of contemporary America, stripping this

once strong nation of its maturation processes; therefore, our country as a
whole suffers from the lack of an adult male identity and the subsequent
inability of all its citizens to achieve maturity and independence.
Consequently, what we find in contemporary America is a loss of "pride of
productivity" in favor of an ever growing population of immature
consumers, ever searching for the metaphorical "mother's breast" – be it the
welfare state, a new car, a pair of celebrity sneakers, or the "feel good"
mentality emanating from a nonjudgmental socialistic state of mind that
believes government should and would take care of you from too
oftentimes "teenaged womb" to even more oftentimes "teenaged tomb."

Without fathers to "wean" them from their dependencies, many
Americans today are unable to achieve identities separate from the
overwhelming maternal mythologies currently eclipsing the patriarchal
social function. These maternal mythologies are the reason the new
"American" emphasis is on the group, not the individual. They are why the
single voice, especially the dissenting voice, is to be scorned and silenced,
and why "good intentions" are more important than excellence of
performance. To them, any means justify the end – if that end wears a
"politically correct" label, that is. And equality is defined as everyone
finishes the same, rather than everyone has the same opportunity. Can you
imagine anyone in America today encouraging youths to be better than
other youths, to strive to "beat" the others, instead of constantly struggling
to make sure we all "get along." Maternal America would be shocked. No
one should be left off the bridge to the twenty-first century. Fathers
wouldn't be shocked. Fathers would want to leave a great number off that
bridge: murderers, drug dealers, thieves, rapists, child molesters – do I have
to go on?

But I'm afraid I've gotten just a little ahead of myself here. Let's go
back a bit. Just what are these "maternal mythologies" I'm talking about,
and why is it important to be weaned from them? And, most importantly,
how do we free ourselves without denigrating mothers, without denigrating
the maternal function, and – ultimately – without denigrating women?
Women have been denigrated enough. Indeed, the devaluation of women
must be stopped. Denigrating women is not part of paternity; at least, it
shouldn't be. Paternity and maternity are equal terms, complements.
Nevertheless, they are, despite their equality, different.

Traditionally, there is a clearly definable and important difference between the maternal and paternal *functions*: Mothers love fully and "unconditionally," while fathers mete out love restrictively and "conditionally." A mother loves her children no matter what they look like or what they achieve – or, most importantly, what they do not achieve. The maternal function is to be nonjudgmental. Her children do not have to earn her love; it is given freely without their even having to ask for it. Picture this scene: A young child awakens early from his or her bed and, rubbing the sleep from his or her eyes, wanders barefoot, clothed only in his or her pajamas, into the kitchen where the aroma of the morning's breakfast is in the air. This child's mother is busily stirring oatmeal at the stove. She senses her child's entrance and turns to see her precious little darling. What does this child have to do to get his or her mother to rush to him or her and be gathered up in mother's loving arms? You know the answer: absolutely nothing! This mother will drop everything to cradle her child, still warm from its long night's sleep, in her embrace. This maternal function, to love unconditionally, is essential to the growth of a child. Children who are loved like this grow up to be confident and successful, especially if – and this is a big "if" – the mother's unconditional love is tempered by the father's conditional way of loving.

Even after she gives birth to her child and the actual umbilical cord is severed, the mother and child are still connected by an exceedingly powerful psychological bond, the proverbial "apron strings," if you will. This is good, for it is during these early, informative years that the child benefits from the mother's unconditional giving and loving. In the mother's embrace, the child feels wanted and adored. The child is nourished and pampered. The child feels safe. The child develops strength and confidence. Yet those same apron strings that bring such succor to the developing child can, with the passage of time, become destructive. The psychological umbilical cord can, itself, strangle and suffocate. Let's go back to the image of the fetus developing in its mother's womb. While the child is protected and nourished by his or her mother's egg, when the "birthing" time comes, that once all important shell must be broken and the umbilical, eventually, severed. If it isn't, the baby will die within, be "still born." Ironically, the once life-sustaining egg becomes itself a suffocating means of destruction. Similarly, the mother's children must be weaned from her metaphorical apron strings in much the same way. The mother's unconditional loving, so essential to the developing child, must be complemented by the paternal "conditional" function, for, as long as the child is "at one" with his or her mother, that child can never develop independently from her. That child cannot mature and find his or her identity as an individual separate from the mother. And, just as importantly, that child cannot discover his or her role in society, away from the maternal family "nest."

But what is the paternal function and how does it work? Why do we need fathers? How did we lose our fathers? And how can we get them back?

IV

The paternal function is, succinctly, to "wean" his children from what the father perceives to be the potentially suffocating and destructive unconditional love of their mother. From the father's point of view, his children cannot gain individuality or develop a sense of societal identity as long as they are still absorbed by the all consuming maternal function. Consequently, to him, the process of maturation is the differentiation of "self" from maternity, that is, the separation of his children from their identification with "mommy." As he perceives it, his children's dependence on their mother is more than a symbiotic "mutualism"; it is the very loss of their autonomy.

When the foetus is in the womb, it is virtually unaware of any difference between its self and its mother; to the developing foetus, mother and self are "one." The mother's body is, in effect, the developing foetus' entire universe. When the baby is born and the umbilical cord is cut, however, the baby takes his or her first step towards beginning the process of developing a physical "self" separate from the mother. In fact, maturation can be seen in terms of a definition of the self as it differentiates its "being" from all else. Succinctly, identity comes, ironically, from recognizing what is *not* you. Yet that newly birthed infant is still barely aware of any differentiation between his or her "self" and mom. And the mother's breast is still a strong point of connection between the two "as one." Nevertheless, the physical process of separation has been set into motion, and the influence of the father has begun.

While the maternal function is focused primarily on the physiological development of children, the paternal function is concerned with the children's *symbolic* development. Thus, while the mother gives her baby the solid nourishment of breast milk, the father gives his newborn infant metaphorical sustenance, in the form of a "name," the name of the father.

Now, it is true that any parent, or anyone for that matter, can name a child. Children in matrilineal societies take their mother's name; however, this practice can usually be traced to very ancient times when people did not realize the connection between sex and pregnancy – probably because of the long gestation period between coitus and birthing – when it was believed that women, alone, produced babies. But this "naming" ritual is, overwhelmingly, in modern western cultures part of the paternal function. For example, whatever one may think of the behavior or of the very idea, the notion that an unmarried pregnant woman will seek a husband before the birth of her child just to give her baby a "name" is quite commonplace and familiar. Additionally, when a woman marries in most western cultures, she traditionally takes her husband's name. I say traditionally because women today, whether they know it or not, are trying desperately to usurp this male function. Contemporary women who refuse, upon marriage, to assume their husband's name or who create hyphenated married names are consciously or unconsciously rebelling against patriarchal control of the "naming" function, for, perhaps, they intuit the great, enormous power inherent in the process. Or, perhaps, they are unconsciously or even consciously clinging to "the name of their own father," the signifier of the father they fear they are about to lose through their matrimony to "another" man. Remember, the great value of the mythopoeic process is that it reveals the "truth" that opposites prove ultimately to be the same. So a woman who rebels against taking her husband's name in marriage is actually validating the primal stature of her father by clinging to his name. And, in her rebellion, when she hyphenates her two last names, she is actually accepting the names of the two men, father and husband.

Nevertheless, what is the significance of this "naming" function of paternity? And why make so much fuss about it?

The baby's name is *both* its first step toward creating an identity separate from its mother and its entrance into the symbolic realm. When a father gives his child a name, the father takes ownership of that child and, thereby, begins the process of separating his child from its mother. Furthermore, by giving the child *his* name, the father opens the way for that child to identify with him; identification with the father is another means of weaning the child away from its mother. Moreover, when the child receives a name, the child receives a "signifier" that separates it from not only the mother but also the "all else." This signifier is a great and "magical" gift, for, as mythology demonstrates over and over again, names are very powerful – symbolically. Think of fairy tales like "Rumplestilskin," where the knowledge of a name gives one power over its owner. And look at what is "at stake" in this fairy tale: the mother's giving away of her newborn child! When you heard or read the story of "Rumplestilskin," did you ever wonder why he would want her child? He could have asked for her love or her riches. It seemed so drastic and inappropriate a demand to ask for her baby, didn't it? Now, do you see why? The tale is a metaphor of the conflict between the maternal and paternal functions; he or she who controls the "name" assumes ownership of the baby.

Mythologies also stress the magical nature of names; for example, Isis gains divine power by tricking Ra into revealing his secret name, for, in ancient Egypt, as in mythologies all over the world, the ultimate name of God cannot be known because it reveals the key to the deity's identity and gives the possessor power over the god, him- or herself. The person and the name are inseparable. In the Isis myth, the Goddess first poisons (with his own dribbling spital) the aged yet all powerful Ra then cures him to discover his true name and, thereby, gain the god's power – not for herself – so she can install it in her *son* Horus. Here, once again, is the metaphorical battle of paternal and maternal functions, and, once again, the female "defeats" the male by gaining knowledge of his name to the benefit of her relationship with her child.

Furthermore, could fairy tales like "Rumplestilskin" and mythologies like the story of Isis really be thinly veiled Oedipal "wish fulfillments"? They certainly do seem like projections from the mind of a child who wishes he or she could negate the dominant father's conditional functioning by transferring his "naming" power to mother, who loves totally and unconditionally – though the children play minimal roles in the tales – but isn't that how displacement works? The child purposely keeps a low profile in the stories to draw attention away from the truth. Or could they be – as I sometimes believe – the "wish fulfillment" fantasies of females, intuiting the inevitable victory of the paternal function over maternity, who wish to reverse the inexorable ill fortunes of fate? Could they be a mother's attempt to wrestle the powerful "naming" function from males?

On the lighter side, as a professor, I have seen the power of the "name" demonstrated, over and over again, on the pages of student notebooks, especially the notebooks of women students. While a good number of my male students are busily carving the word "boring" on their desk tops, many of my female students, perhaps intuiting the power inherent in the paternal "naming" function, will be, instead, constantly scribbling the name of their beloved "significant other" all over their note pages when they are (supposedly) listening to my lectures. So what are these young women doing? And why are they doing it? It seems they are doing two separate types of name scribbling. The first type consists of the linking of their names with the names of their boyfriends; for example, if a girl's first name is "Susan" and her beloved's last name is "Smith," she will explore the possible combination of the two by writing "Susan Smith" or "Sue Smith" or "Mrs. Susan Smith" – over and over again. Is this her acceptance of his name for her and for her potential children? Is this her recognition of the paternal "naming" function? And what of the second type of name scribbling? What is it? In this instance, she will write only *his* name, again repeatedly – over and over. What is she trying to accomplish here? This type of scribbling seems, itself, to have two functions. First, by knowing and repeatedly reproducing his name, she gains a power of "possession." Her constant scribbling of his name represents and reaffirms their "connection" and the fact that she – of all people – "knows" him best. Remember the mythological Egyptian notion that the knowledge of a person's name gives one power over that person because it reveals his or her identity, for he or she is inseparable from his or her name? She's a contemporary Isis, reproducing that ancient myth in the "here and now."

Second, his name is a *substitute* for him. When she writes his name, she is, in a sense, bringing him to her. She is silently reciting a "spell" designed to close the great spacial and temporal gap that has currently come between them. Though she desperately wants to be with him, he is not there – at least, not physically. Consequently, the repeated scribbling of his name is a ritual designed to dissolve time and space, so she can embrace her beloved, there in the classroom, even though he may be miles away. Through this "spell," she can be with him symbolically, repeatedly recreating him through the repetition of his name. If she cannot be with him physically, she can, at least, be with him even if it is "in name only." Think of it. Our names are substitutes for ourselves. Our names have the power of making us materialize, either physically or in the mind's eye. When someone calls my name, that person has a power over me, for chances are – if I hear the summoning – I will answer, even out of a deep sleep. And, if I don't, I am still there, visualized, in that person's consciousness. My name creates my image in his or her mind.

Consequently, when my female students scribble the names of their boyfriends, they are intuitively recognizing the importance of our symbolic identities and the paternal function that gives us access to them. They are experiencing a true mythological process, one occurring in the "here and now" in demonstration of the "living" nature of mythology. Yet, perhaps, the most powerful *contemporary* recognition of the paternal "naming" function is the brilliant and enlightened creation of the Vietnam Memorial, where the names of that war's fallen heroes and heroines are carved (not scribbled) in stone. But simply carving their names in stone does not make a memorial. Look at the word "memorial" itself; at root, it means "of or relating to memory." Consequently, a memorial, that is, a commemoration, is most successful when it fulfills *all* shades of its meaning – in this case to be, at once, a monument to our lost loved ones as well as a vehicle to bring them back to our memories. The Vietnam Memorial *is* both. The surface of the dark stone is highly polished, so, when one gazes at a name carved into the wall, one's own image is superimposed. Thus, the name of the lost beloved is "at one" with the image of the grieving lover. Because of the "reflective" – think of all the meanings of the word reflective: "to think back" as well as "to reproduce the image of" – nature of the wall, the name appears, literally, to be carved into the "reflection" of the person staring at it, as that person is in the process of, simultaneously, "reflecting" on the name. In this way, the living and the dead become one, thereby negating the potential for victory of either over the other. They are complements of one soul mythologically transcending life and death. Thus, the Vietnam Memorial is itself alive. Every time visitors stare at its multitudinous legion of names, they give their "lives," as have the fallen warriors before them – in both meanings of "before them," that is "previous to them" and the names "in front of their eyes" – back to that memorial and all its names. Their "reflections" (their images in the polished stone) animate – give life to – the names on the wall, while, at the same time, the names on the wall animate the nature of their "reflections" (their thoughts). This is why, to me, the "wall" is a *living* mythology, for it illustrates the "sameness" of opposites while it "bridges" the concrete reality of the current moment and its tragic sense of loss, its recognition of the separateness of "self" and "other," with the eternal reality of the mythopoeic, hermetic realm where lovers are atoned, "at one" – and it does so through its recognition of the transcendent powers inherent in the "name."

Thus, just as we are born from the mother physically, we are born from the father symbolically. When we are born through the father, we are born a "second time," into a nonmaterial, abstract existence – a world of ideas and possibilities, a metaphorical consciousness that eclipses maternal matter. Through the paternal "naming" function, we enter the symbolic realm of language, the structuring nature of which creates a psychological domain, an alternative "subtle" reality to the purely physiological, concrete world of the mother. Consequently, through language, the father goes beyond mere physical paternity to become "guarantor of the law" and, ultimately, progenitor of culture. The father gives birth to us; through him, we are weaned from mother and family to enter society – the society he has *himself* constructed; so, ultimately, from him, we learn our identity and place in the structure of the culture he has created. Furthermore, once we enter his concept of society, his conditional love sets rules and regulations, norms of behavior, which he imposes and maintains through his signifying function as the "guarantor of the law." Therefore, when he dictates, "as long as you live under my roof, you'll do as I say," he is simply declaring his patriarchal function in the society he has envisioned. When his children enter his house, they exit the mother and are, thus, reborn through him. He matures them by releasing them from their dependency upon the mother, and, once independent of her, each of his children is free to earn – through him – an identity of his or her own. In short, it is the father's primary function to bring his birthed children to mature individuation – *all* his birthed children, sons and daughters alike – but especially his sons, for there *is* a difference between sons and daughters. They are *equal* – yes – but *different*.

V

Because daughters are subject to a "natural" process of metamorphosis into womanhood, they are, through this almost "magical happening," literally "overtaken" by nature. As females, they are "at one" with nature. They *are* nature. They are what "it" is all about. As famed comparative mythologist Joseph Campbell insightfully quipped, they *are* "it." They are the "givers" of life. Through their wombs, life is born. By the milk of their breasts, life is nurtured and sustained. They are the vehicles of life, the "begin all" and the "end all."

Among what we incorrectly label as "primitive" cultures throughout the world, there is a recognition of this "giving" feminine nature. When a girl begins her first menstruation cycle, she is isolated, removed from her society, so she can turn inward to intuitively "feel" and, thereby, come to understand what is happening *to* her because it does happen to her; it overtakes her. She sits alone in a remote hut and contemplates what her "change" from girlishness to womanhood means. She reflects upon the "giving" nature of her physical body. She realizes it is the very function of her physiology to be "giving." In this way, she identifies with the Goddess mother of us all, for Her power is the power of fertility, of giving life and of sustaining it. Isis is the "throne" of her son Horus; that is, she "supports" him in every imaginable way.

Ultimately, the Goddess even gives birth to the gods themselves. The "Mother of the Gods" is a common mythological theme, visible everywhere, all over the world, in all generations. Therefore, She, the Goddess, is the "eternal" feminine. Consequently, the daughter, as she begins her cycles of menstruation, meditates on the great mystery of her identification with this all encompassing Goddess. What the daughter comes to realize is that each woman is herself the incarnation of the Goddess. Each woman is herself the giver and continuer of life. From this perspective, woman is identified as the great "transformer." Through her womb, mortal life is made infinite. When she accepts the seed of her man, her womb "transforms" that seed into his children, into the next generation. She transforms the finite, mortal quality of a single male life into generational immortality. She transforms her husband into their children, one man into the next generation. In this way, in this "return" to the womb, mortal man is made immortal through the propagation of his species. Thus, womb is tomb. This is why world mythologies predominantly equate the god of sex with the god of death. He "dies" in her womb, so his children can be born. Metaphorically, the male is sacrificed to her function. Oedipus blinds himself because he was himself blind to the metaphorical nature of this "truth." Men serve life; women are life.

We may come to believe, then, the daughter does not need her father or his paternal function. We may conclude, since her feminine maturity is a "natural" process of womanhood and reproductivity that overtakes her, she needs no external male factor to bring her to independence. But she does. The daughter needs the father to bring her to maturity – not physically as a reproductive creature – psychically and metaphorically, to help "awaken" in her a sense of *self* and of identity apart from her natural physiology, so she is not *overwhelmed* by her "giving" nature or by *nature* itself. Because nature has fashioned her to be giving, she can lose herself in her own giving nature. She can give too much and inappropriately in the mistaken notion that giving is itself always the right thing to do in every situation. Because she is so giving, she can mistakenly believe "giving" is the way to be loved and appreciated and that, if she isn't always giving, there is something wrong with her femininity. Without fathers, she can misconstrue her giving female physiology with her personal female psyche. Because her body is fashioned by nature to be giving, she may believe that her whole being, her "self," is also designed to be constantly giving or, worse, to be "given away." Tragically, without fathers, her giving nature becomes mixed up with the giving away of her "self." Giving life does not mean giving away one's *own* life. The power to give life identifies her with the Goddess. The giving away of her own life leaves her with no identity.

Consequently, the father's function is always the same, regardless of whether his children are male or female. After all, don't mothers give birth to sons and daughters, alike. Therefore, the life of the daughter, like the life of the son, must also be allowed to individuate from the mother. Just as sons need to be reborn into the symbolic realm, so too do daughters. Thus, it is the father's function to awaken in his daughters – just as he does with his sons – a sense of "self" and confidence in their lives as individuals, so they learn to give "conditionally" and, more importantly, so they learn to keep a little bit of themselves for themselves. The father teaches his daughter that it is "all right" for her to not give completely and unconditionally, that it is "all right" to not drown in her maternal function, so she can enjoy a little bit of life for herself rather than function merely and totally as a "vehicle" of life, a too often unappreciated "stage" through which life passes. In short, it is the father's role to oppose her nature and "nature" itself. He gives her an individual "name" to separate her from the Goddess, whose faceless "thousand names" swallow up all femininity. Ultimately, it is the father's role to replace natural law with his societal law, so, when his daughter enters into a relationship with a man, she has the confidence and intelligence to know she is an individual. The father teaches his daughter that she doesn't "give" to the man for the sake of giving; rather, when she gives, she is to give to the relationship, for the sake of the relationship, thereby bringing to balance the enigmatical and mythical $1 + 1 = 1$ equation, whose solution is not only woman (1) plus man (1) equals baby (1) but also the woman (1) plus the man (1) equals the "marriage" (1) of the two into one, not the sacrifice of the woman (1 turned to 0) + 1 (the man) = 1 (the man) equation. Through the paternal function, daughters learn there is a difference between giving unconditionally and giving restrictedly, that is, appropriately and wisely.

Without fathers, a daughter may give her "all" to a man only to find there is nothing in her relationship with him – even though she's given and given. Let's use this analogy to explain: Think of a relationship between a man and a woman as a joint bank account. If she gives everything directly to her man instead of depositing it in their joint account, when she goes to the joint account, what will she find in their metaphorical "bank book"? Nothing. Likewise, if she gives everything to the man, when he wants more – because he'll always want more – and turns to her to get it, what will she have to give? Nothing. So where will he go? To another woman? Very possibly. Almost assuredly. Therefore, to help his daughter avoid this emotional "bankruptcy," the father tempers (even stifles) his daughter's giving nature, so she learns to give to the relationship "joint account" instead of directly to her man. So, when her man wants more, even if she's given her all, she can go with him to their account, and it, the relationship account, will be full, filled with all she's given – even if he hasn't given a proverbial "plugged nickle".

It is a drastic understatement to say the father/daughter relationship is a *difficult* process. It is *more* than difficult! We have only begun to, allow me this cliche, "scratch the surface" here. For, as we shall shortly come to see, to daughters, the father's "law" is a "double-edged" sword that "cuts both ways," positively and negatively. What he perceives as a constructive "reeling in" of her behavior, especially her sexual behavior, she may perceive as a tampering with, or even a restriction of, her sexual freedom. You see, the moment she becomes a sexual creature, her sexuality puts her in direct conflict with her father's notion of society.

But more, much more, on this later, for now let us explore the father/son relationship a little bit.

VI

Goethe once wisely remarked, "With girls we love what they are. With young men, what they promise to be." We love the feminine for what it is, "giving." The female gives life. The female even gives of her physical body to sustain and nurture life. The female is giving. The male, conversely, is *not*. Men are selfish. That is their nature. In fact, that is their "natural" inclination. In nature, men have two roles, both of which are supporting functions: If the female *is* life, then the male's purpose is to provide for and to protect that life. Consequently, to carry out those duties, men are aggressive by design. They are made to "take." Nature provides them with physically strong bodies, powerful torsos. Even the quickest of glances demonstrates that the male body is dramatically different from the female body. Their muscle development is different – so too are their hormonal balances. Men are designed to provide and to protect. They must be consistent in their emotions. They hunt. They know where the food sources are, and they actively pursue them. And, by nature's design, men will even wage war to gather up new females or to protect the ones they have. Therefore, it is only "natural" for men to be aggressive and to "take." Nature makes them this way. Selfishness, aggression and taking are *natural* masculine traits. But what is good for nature is often not good for an ordered society – or, surprisingly, for individuals.

Nature is concerned with the strength of dominant males and the passing of their genes, through the "transformational" female womb, to create the next generation. Therefore, nature encourages these males to fulfill their function to the utmost. The ultimate male, in nature, is "alpha male," whose ability to provide for and protect the females is far superior to the lesser skills of his peers. Under this system, what makes a male attractive to females, in fact, is their perception of his ability to successfully carry out these male duties; consequently, strength and power are attractive masculine traits, for they display male functional promise and potential for the propagation of the species. Now, this type of physically "aggressive" man may satisfy nature's generational perspective, for he can pass on his "superior" genes through his impregnation of numerous females – all of whom he feeds and protects thanks to his strength and "selfish" desires, sexual or otherwise – but his "selfishness" is in direct antithesis to the satisfaction of individuals other than himself, especially individual females or other, less dominant, males.

Consequently, in order for a greater number of males and females to "bond" as individuals in mutually satisfying relationships rather than a single-male dominated harem, what is needed is an organized system especially designed to *oppose* nature, particularly the selfish male nature and, just as importantly, what is also needed is a "guarantor" of the laws of this "unnatural" cultural system to ascertain that everyone involved – especially dominant young males, who are quick to abuse the system and the females – obeys the rules. The system is society. The "guarantor of the law" of that societal system is the father.

For society's sake, young men must be *taught* to be submissive and to give to something bigger than themselves. The father's societal law must be forcibly installed in place of the son's "natural" selfishness. This exclusively human process is, in fact, what separates us from the rest of the animal kingdom, where no such civilizing paternal process is evident. Look around us at all the animals and flowers and plants. They are totally atoned with, "at one" – for that is literally what atone means, at one – with, nature. They exhibit none of our human rebellion. They have no sense of mortality – of life and death, no sense even of time and space. They are, in a way, living in Eden before the "fall," a timeless paradise not entrapped by any one place, any one concept of "here and now." They accept nature, are lost in it. They do not experience our human sense of self, our need to find an individuality. Life itself, nature itself, eclipses the individual. The individual is sacrificed to the entity of nature, perpetual nature, whose only rule is "survival of the fittest" – not to the benefit of that "fittest" individual – for the betterment of the "whole" eternal "natural" process. In nature, there is no difference between the lion and the lamb, there is no waiting for a time when the lion will be made to lie down with the lamb. In nature, that "blissful" time is now. The lion does lie down with the lamb – when it's eating it! But don't fret, for nothing is happening. Life is simply being ingested by life, an eternal process of life renewing itself. This wider perspective of life is nature and the maternal function.

The father's function is, conversely, to make *all* his sons "fit" and all his sons fit to *serve* society. This is the father's role, to teach his sons this "truth," to help his sons mature by bringing his boys to the realization that manhood in society includes the giving of one's self to something "bigger" – for example, *commitment* in a relationship – so his boys can, in that way, achieve individual identities. In short, the father must turn his sons away from the "self" love that is fostered and nourished by the unconditional maternal function, so they can "identify" with him and, thereby, with the paternal function itself. While daughters are in constant danger of drowning their concept of "self" in the maternal function, sons must be dragged "kicking and screaming" to the water's edge of "Lake Paternity." Sons must be "forced" to give up the self to a greater cause. In this sense, heroes, who do just that, are made not born – they are made by fathers.

Ultimately, by extension, the father/son relationship is central to the development and maintenance of societal "laws" because it is the father who is responsible – no, and this is an important distinction, it is the paternal *function* that is responsible – for the maturation of young males and, subsequently, for their acceptance by, and the finding of their place in, society. In contemporary America, the importance of this maturation process has been, tragically, lost. Conversely, however, in what we erroneously label as "primitive" societies, this male maturation process is explicit and well defined. In these so-called "primitive" types of societies, the male rites of passage are well-structured, traumatic and transforming experiences. In contrast to the peaceful isolation and meditation their sisters undergo, the young boys are put through physically trying and punishing rituals – for the good of society.

As these "primitive" young boys age, they become progressively aggressive. This physical assertiveness may be only "natural" to these young males; however, it cannot be tolerated for the orderly existence and survival of the tribe. At this stage of development, the older boys, taking advantage of their superior bodily size and strength, begin to push around the girls and younger boys, so it is at this point, when the aging boys become too much for their mothers to handle, that the adult males are called upon to turn these uncontrollable youths into mature, responsible adults and productive members of their society. To achieve this, the men put the young "initiates" through enormously brutal, oftentimes violent and purposefully disfiguring, trials, making the boys suffer *physically* and *visibly*. After undergoing these maturation processes, the boys are reborn in new men's bodies, so – once through the process – their former bodies must now demonstrate visible, tangible signs of their transformational rebirth: scaring, disfigurement, subincision and circumcision, tattooing, etc. This powerful symbolical and physical metamorphosis is such an essential ritual that no one, especially no mother, would dare come between the boys and the adult males, no matter how much the boys may be made to suffer or be forced to endure. In fact, the entire tribe is a part of the male maturation process simply because the "civilizing" of these wild young boys is beneficial to every member of the clan.

Here is an illustrative scenario: On the night designated for the ritual, the men come for the boys. The men appear "magical," mystical and ferocious. They bleed themselves and use their own shed men's blood as a glue to cover their bodies with feathers, fur tufts, even plant shards – anything to make them appear fierce, menacing and "other worldly." Their entrance is marked by the penetrating screams of noise-makers, like the bull-roarers which they swing around their heads, to make a great and bone-chilling racket. Understandably, the boys are petrified and cling to their mothers, but now mothers are no longer able to protect them. The women may pretend to help but, in reality, their show of opposition is just that, a "show." From this night on, the males take control. The young boys are being taught a lesson: Maternity (nature) is, from this moment – the moment of their entrance into society – subservient to the paternal function. This is, indeed, the central theme. "Primitive" societies are ripe, in fact, with mythologies that explain how the men, who were once ruled by, and under the power of, their females, rebelled and overthrew the oppressive feminine dominance. Obviously, it is hoped, these are not tales to be taken literally. It is more than highly probable that there never was such a time or such a war between men and women. Rather, these mythologies are metaphors, perhaps of male warrior gods usurping the powers of the earlier Goddess tradition, but more likely of the inevitable eclipsing of the maternal function (nature) by the paternal (society). To me, the male victory over the female is symbolic of the father's ultimate weaning of his children away from what he perceives as their mother's suffocating, unconditional love.

So the women retreat and, once in the clutches of the men, the young boys are transformed and "reborn." Here is where they are scarified, tattooed, circumcised, even subincised. Here, they are often forced to endure serious life-threatening peril and may even be abused to the point of experiencing a not so symbolical "death." Some may *not* survive the ordeals. So why is all this done? There is, of course, a reasonable explanation for all this "torture." Just as their sisters begin to shed menstrual blood in expression of their maturation, and in preparation for the pains of the child birthing experience that await them as women, the boys too must undergo a similar bloodletting and painful "rebirthing" experience. Like their sisters, who are undergoing a physical body change, the boys too must have their physical bodies altered. So, when the ordeal is over, the boys who do survive are no longer uncontrollable youths. Their boys' bodies are physically changed. They are reborn, resurrected, in new men's bodies. (In a way, doesn't this explain the great populatity of body-piercing and tatooing so widespread amoung contempoary American youths?) This process may sound cruel and barbaric to us. And, perhaps, it is. However, these ritualized young boys are now mature males, adults, accepted and respected members of their tribe, who know their place in its society. They are identified as men and, more importantly, they have identified with the male "civilizing," paternal function.

The need for young boys to undergo a maturation process is so essential to the male psyche that many of the adult members of these tribes sometimes voluntarily put themselves through the maturation ordeals numerous times, simply to reaffirm their masculinity. Older males will undergo the process of subincision, where the penis is cut open from the base upwards to the tip, on more than one ceremonial occasion. Why? To create the "male womb." Remember, the boys are being *reborn* here. They were born once through the female womb, and now they are being born again – this time through the male womb. They are no longer their mother's children. They are now their father's children. Because this second birth is essentially symbolical, however, it pales, physiologically, in comparison to the boy's actual first birth, so every effort is made by the adult males in the tribe to make this ritual as comparable in its physical nature as possible to the female birthing process. Additionally, because males are "selfish," it is most likely they will not voluntarily give up the greedy pleasures of that selfishness in favor of what they perceive as the "compromises" of society; consequently, the boys must be physically "abused" in order to wean them from the gratifications of their selfish natures. Succinctly, and literally, they must be "beaten into submission."

Before we panic and totally reject the brutal nature of these "primitive" rituals, allow me to make a rather outlandish statement: Young males reach a time in their lives when they are actually *ready* and even anxious to undergo such challenging and painful self-defacing processes as these maturation rites. No, they are not masochists. Something else is going on, and I think I have a little idea of what it is. I believe there is some jealousy of females at work here. Because nature "overtakes" females and nature is a very physical process, feminine maturation is quite visible: Females begin a menstruation cycle. Women receive a visible, physical "sign." But men do not have a comparable notification; therefore, men are never really sure when they have matured. This male need to have, as Othello so aptly phrased it, "ocular proof" of their masculinity is what drives their need to be "wounded" or, to put it more bluntly and accurately, "wombed." Think of Stephen Crane's insightful coming-of-age novel of the Civil War, *The Red Badge of Courage*. What is the red badge? It is the open wound, the bleeding "scar," the need for a male womb. It is the sign, earned through battle, that tells a man and all other men and women that he is, indeed, a "man." Zeus, the father of the gods, gives birth to Dionysus through such a womb, and patriarchal Odysseus, returned home after his epic journey, is recognized by son Telemachus by the same kind of wound in the thigh. Apparently, or perhaps obviously, ownership of such a wound – or male womb – is the ocular proof of a male's maturity and, thereby, his right to claim the paternal, "warrior" role. All males possess a phallus. Only the *father* has the "male womb," through which his children can find their second birthing.

But a male cannot just "inherit" a womb, as females do. He has to earn it. His womb must be a warrior's wound. He must suffer. He must feel the pain. And his wound must be greater than the wound of the female. He must, as a man, outdo her bleeding. He must outdo her suffering. His wound must eclipse her womb. Isn't this why warriors, to earn their warrior rank, undergo brutal rituals of physical endurance – torture and self-torture? You bet it is! I'm reminded of a Hemingway short story, "The Indian Camp," where a young boy accompanies his physician father across the river to a Native American settlement in order to assist his father with the birthing of a squaw's baby. All through her delivery, the squaw's warrior husband is in the bunk bed above his wife, listening all throughout the night to the great pain she is suffering undergoing childbirth. Her ordeal is particularly complicated, for she is forced to endure the birth of a breech baby via a Caesarean section, performed without anesthetic. In the morning, when the baby is finally born, they find the young warrior-husband dead in his upper bunk. He has slit his own throat. Why? His self-inflicted death wound was the only way he could "best" his wife's painfully excruciating experience of childbirth. The warrior realized his wife's "natural" function was a far more physically painful challenge than anything he had to endure to be considered a man, so, by his own definition, she was a better "man" than he was. He had lost his manhood in light of her birthing ordeal. He felt emasculated. He had to outdo her suffering to get back his manhood. Ironically, as his wife gives a life – his child, he takes one away – his own. And he had to do it! You see, his suicide is his final effort to rid himself of male "selfishness." He had to outdo her pain and outdo her life-giving function by "giving" the ultimate sacrifice: the brutal taking of his own life. Ironically, now that his child was born, he (our young warrior) – not she (his squaw wife) – had to maintain possession of the womb.

Consequently, there comes a time in a boy's psyche when he feels he is *ready* to sacrifice, to undergo the male maturation rituals, no matter how painful or horrific they may prove to be. As an aging male professor, I find myself, more and more, being cast into a father/son relationship with many of my young male students, for a great deal of them are "without fathers," so they are forced to seek the substitute paternity of strangers. I mention this because I cannot even begin to count the number of times the following scenario has been played out in my office: I'm busily at work lost in some scholarly tome or wasteful bureaucratic report when, sensing someone in the doorway, I look up to gaze into the beaming smile of one of my young male students. "Hey, Doc," he says with a new energy in his voice, "you'll never guess what I just did." I don't have to guess. I know *exactly* what he did. But I would never "steal his thunder," by letting on. Instead, I smile back weakly and say, "I don't know. Tell me." Then the words I've heard countless times before from others just like him fill my office afresh from the newfound power in this young man's voice, "I've joined the Army!" Of course. I knew it. You knew it. He has reached that point in his life when the selfishness of male youth has become tiresome. He wants to earn his wound, the "sign" that he is ready to assume the paternal function and wrest the womb from the female who has had possession of it all too long. But, without a father, he has no means to maturation – no means, that is, except, he believes, the military. In the Army, he will endure basic training, "boot camp," where his clinging to the "self" will be beaten out of him, replaced by the concept of giving to something bigger than himself.

Perhaps, this is a good place to discuss the function of the military and why our current attitudes about it are furthering the destruction of American masculinity. As you can readily surmise from the above, one of the perceived roles of the military is to mature young men. Tragically, in fact, the military has become a father substitute and an apparently necessary one in light of the father absence we are now being forced to endure. However, this is not – was never intended to be – and should not be the military's role. The military should be concerned with providing protection for the society it represents. Whatever you may think of the processes, the military should seek out and destroy our enemies as well as protect our borders. If it is properly carrying out its function, the military is a destructive force, a killing machine. The military should not have to be concerned with the socializing of youths, especially boys. *Fathers* should be maturing males and preparing them for the rigors of military duty. When males join the military, they should already be mature men. The Marines, for example, ask for a "few good men"; they don't say come to us, and we'll turn you into a good man. No, they want the "proud, the tested, the true." Nevertheless, what we see today are vast numbers of boys seeking military service because they *believe* the military is their last hope for maturation. And, frighteningly enough, in most cases it is! To make the situation even worse, more and more females are turning to the military because, without fathers, they too are beginning to seek alternative vehicles for identification. But the military is not the answer. The military is not designed to mature individuals. So don't look to the military for maturation.

In fact, just look at what all this misguided immaturity is doing to our military. Sexual harassment is one major problem – and a serious one, perhaps not even the most serious. Who knows what difficulties lie ahead. Like our media, like our education system, like our entertainment industry before it, our military is now being "deconstructed" and, thereby, weakened and ineffective. Nevertheless, whatever future failures our military may face, the "sex scandals" we see in today's military are not a reflection on the military; they are the results of a failed civilian social system. These sex offenders come to the military and thrive because of civilian tampering with the military systems. This is one problem that has been transplanted *on* to the military. But, unfortunately, there are others. The military is not a socializing organization. It was never meant to be one. The military cannot mature men or women, for that matter, so social problems are becoming more and more hurtful to all involved because men and women are being thrown together in potentially volatile situations *before* they are ready to deal with such intimacy and before the necessary bonds of trust, that come with maturity, have been able to form. If you think about it, the military today is forcing boys and girls together, putting weapons in their hands, and giving some (sometimes, simply because of seniority) authority and power over others. Does that sound right to you? Let's return to those "primitive" peoples again. In these primitive societies, warriors – almost always *males* – live apart from the women. These warriors hunt during peacetime and battle during times of conflict. And, remember, before these warriors could earn the revered "name" of warrior and carry a weapon, they had to undergo an ordeal at the hands of their fathers to earn that maturity of rank and the respect it carries in their society. The process, and the idea behind it, is a simple one: Because the very existence of the tribe depends upon the successful functioning of its warriors (its military), it is essential that warriors (soldiers) be mature *before* they assume such an essential role. And what is that role? To kill and defeat the enemy. Can it be any clearer than this?

So what are we doing to our military? We've made a fine mess of it, haven't we? We've silenced the constructive paternal voice to embrace a deconstructive effeminate tone, so most of the time our military is in a United Nations peace-keeping or humanitarian role; we ship them overseas, so they can handout food while they stand around, dodging bullets, hoping to not get shot. Meanwhile, as they keep an eye out for major battles, daily atrocities are being carried out right under their noses. People are killed in the alleyways while United Nations planes fly a thousand feet overhead, reporting clear skies and quiet conditions. Look, the answer is obvious: Either we accept our military and, more importantly, respect it for what it *is*

– our warriors, trained to kill and defeat our enemies – or we end it, period, and accept the consequences of our persistent and blind rejection of all things *male* – like the male function of protecting our society and defeating our enemies rather than enduring and appeasing those antagonists who seek our destruction. Otherwise, before we know it, our military will be out selling cookies door-to-door like the girl scouts to raise money to ransom our country from those who will oppose and hold it prisoner. I cannot stress this enough: The military is not an organ for maturing males, or is it an arena for women to find identities.

I shake his hand, this young man who stands in my doorway for, perhaps, the final time, and "congratulate" him. "Good luck," my words sound wrong, phony, even to me. He leaves, and I worry about him – not because of the military, *per se*. I am, myself, a Vietnam-era veteran. I'm not afraid of military service or the potential of combat. I worry, for I fear he is driven to it because it is his *only* hope, his *only* way. I worry for him and all the males in this nation. What ways do they have of maturing? Without fathers, what hope do they have? Men have been emasculated in contemporary America – at least, the paternal function has. Oh, there's plenty of "machismo," plenty of male posturing. Just look at our so-called athletes, especially the "bad boys." They're part of the problem, too. But where are the real fathers who will give these young males and young women, too, a second birth, so they can be reborn, these young boys, as men – these young girls, as women? And, perhaps, I worry too because he has thought enough of me to come tell me of his plans. Is this *my* sign? Don't forget, I, too, am a male with no visible means of maturation. Yet I can't help but believe his coming to say "goodbye" is a recognition of my possession of the paternal function. Does he see me as a father? Do I possess the male womb? Is this his one last way of asking me to do my male duty and, in a sense, "adopt" him? And, if so, should I have let him go, or should I have taken on, as an adult male, the responsibility of his maturation myself – even though I am a remote and unsatisfactory substitute for a real father? I don't know. I just don't know.

"Good luck. Keep in touch." The words echo, over and over again, in my head, "good luck," "good luck," saddening me greatly because I don't know for whom they are meant – him, me, or America.

VII

What happens when a culture loses its male maturation rites? Just look around. Watch the news on television. Read the headlines of our local papers. What do you see? Destructive adolescents and arrested adolescence everywhere: drugs, promiscuity, violence, anti-social behavior, an unhealthy concern with "self." As Joseph Campbell once put it, you see a people who have lost their mythologies. You see young people who do not know how to live in, or how to behave in, society. You see youths and immature adults, who rape, steal, and murder. Yet, to me, what is even more frightening is the lack of remorse or conscience of today's criminal element. Ask any police officer. Those "on the job" will tell you. What we face in contemporary America is a very different breed of rapist, a very different kind of murderer. When you look into the eyes of today's criminal element, you see no sense of empathy for their victims, no hint of regret for whatever crime these thugs may have committed. You don't see evidence of any mythological epiphany that all of us are "one," no sense of any kind of "golden rule," no idea that what you do to the other you do to yourself. Therefore, when you consider an inordinately great amount of crime, especially violent crime, is committed by male youths, can you now be surprised? Of course not. It is obvious. We have failed to bring these boys to maturation. What's worse, our young women are following the same destructive path. How can a "girl" give birth to a baby and flush it down a toilet or stuff it in a dumpster? How can a young mother sit by or even assist her "lover of the day" to molest or beat her children? And why does she have so many children from so many different lovers – many of whom (lovers and children alike) she doesn't even know? But, worst of all, why do we try to understand them? Why do we make excuses for their behavior, condone their behavior? Why? Why do we *take* it?

And we call ourselves civilized! The so-called primitive society we perceive to be inferior to our own is actually a far more efficient, effective and beneficial social system because it is structured around a patriarchal maturation process that allows its members, especially its young males, to become productive members of its society and to know their place in it. The "primitive" society affords its young men with mythologies and identities. A young man earns his name and role within his society based on his performance within its well-defined structure. In some of these "primitive" cultures, in fact, a boy does not even get a name until he "earns" it by killing an enemy warrior and taking the name of the vanquished. But don't get derailed by the horror of such a ritual; it is just an extreme example to prove a point. The idea is males reach maturity by accepting the challenges imposed on them by adult males. The adult males, as guarantors of the law of their tribe, set the norms of the trial – the ordeals – the young boys must successfully complete as well as the laws they must live by from then on. The rules are clear and simple: If you succeed, you are a man, and as a man you must follow a prescribed set of norms. This "primitive" conditional process reveals the paternal function.

Without fathers, we – the "civilized" – are, conversely, channeling our youths into group structures that are quickly becoming isolated from the rest of society. Look how we label entire generations: "baby boomers" or "generation X," whose very names illustrate their inability to "grow up" or their tragic loss of identity. And the "grouping" doesn't stop there. America is a polarized nation. What has become of the phrase, "I am an American"? Who says that anymore? No one. Why not? Because everyone has become hyphenated, a member of a "group": African-American, Hispanic-American, Native-American. Apply for a job. Try to get admitted to a college. What is one of the first items on the application form? It's a grid designed to identify you as a member of one of a number of ethnic groups. Nowadays, the individual doesn't apply for a job or to a school. The applicant is, rather, a member of a group, and it is as this group representative that the applicant is either accepted or rejected. As horrible as these examples may be, they are nothing compared to the extreme problems group consciousness creates. This group mentality finds its most destructive form in the rising scourge of "gang" membership America is currently experiencing. When young males cannot find identities as individuals, they seek identities through membership in a gang, for the gang has, ironically enough, an individual personality, which a gang member adopts as his or her own. Allow me to, once again, draw an analogy from my teaching experience. Even though a class is made up of a number of students, each class takes on an identity of its own. For example, I might teach two sessions of the very same course, "Myth, Dream, and Image," yet the experience will be very different with each group. The different students in each class come together to create a "collective" personality, so much so that, when I am teaching each session, I do not even feel I am teaching the same course twice, for the dynamics of each group's "individual" personality radically changes the pedagogical experience.

The question that comes out of all this is interesting: If males have lost the maturation process inherent in the paternal function and are, now, identifying with the "unconditional" nature of the maternal function, why are gangs so violent and anti-female? Wouldn't young males raised under such strong feminine principles assimilate that womanly consciousness and be less violent and more empathetic to their female counterparts? You would think so, wouldn't you. But, much to the dismay of the social engineers who wish to achieve just such a "blending" of the genders, the answer is obviously and resoundingly "no!" And there are a number of reasons why. The most important, however, is the "natural" cause, so we'll explore that. Remember, young girls are "overtaken" by nature. Their physical bodies are literally made for giving. They give birth. They give the very milk of their breasts to nurture life. Consequently, their physiology influences their identity. Because they give openly and freely, they also accept in the same manner. They accept openheartedly without judgment – even their enemies. In fact, it is by nature's design that women should be attracted to those outside of their group, so, in that way, gene pools are diversified; therefore, it is almost always the woman – "sleeping with the enemy" – who falls in love with the so-called sworn "enemy" of her people, who sees no difference between her world and the world of his people, who reaches out to accept all life as equal.

Conversely, young males are not overtaken by nature. They are never "one" with its unconditional acceptance of all life as "equal." Rather, males are built to *serve* nature. When a male enters into a relationship with a female, his is merely a supporting role. He is to provide for her and protect her, so she can carry out her maternal function. Consequently, his body is designed to perform his duties. Remember, his body is strong and equipped for "taking." He hunts and he wars. Thus, his psyche is influenced by his physiology – just as hers is. Therefore, no matter what conditioning he is put through, his physiological function will rear its "ugly" head: He will take! He will be *selfish*. He will compete with and try to defeat others. When the paternal function is in place, however, the "natural" boy will be forcibly shapened by the father, the way a blacksmith's strong, well placed blows shape his product, to channel a boy's natural propensity for taking, that is, his "selfishness," into societally constructive usages. In this way, the boy forced to become a mature male will make a commitment to the female he loves while, simultaneously, fulfilling the tenets of his natural physiology. Ironically, he will still "take," only his taking will be a constructive process for him and his mate; for example, he will go out and earn a living to support his wife and children. He will "take" *for* his family. His warrior nature will be channeled into productive outlets for him and his "tribe." Without fathers, however, the boy's taking nature goes unchecked and often runs destructively amok – this is why boys raised solely under the maternal function are never weaned from their selfishness and do not, for the most part, develop respect and empathy for women.

This scene is inevitable: A boy is raised only by his mother – without a father. Increasingly, the closeness of their mother/son relationship is threatened by his, the son's, aggressive nature. The mother realizes, no matter what she does, she is losing control of her son. He is rebelling against her more and more everyday. His behavior is becoming difficult to bear or to even tolerate. Outside the home, he is misbehaving, sometimes severely so. He may even be a criminal, a violent criminal. He lies to her. He is becoming a stranger. She feels she does not even know the son to whom she gave birth. For his part, when he's at home, an anger is growing in him. He is rejecting her. He feels she suffocates him. Then, one day, he explodes. If she is lucky, it is just words – ugly, nasty, hurtful words. Too often, though, she is not, and it becomes physical. He strikes her. He brutally strikes his mother.

You see, unfortunately, what is lost in the lives of these young males being raised without fathers is not their aggressive "taking" natures; mothers are not neutralizing that selfish masculinity by raising their sons "unisexually" or by trying to instill in them respect for women. Rather, what is lost is the means of controlling that potentially hurtful selfishness to effect societally productive ends. This is why boys raised without the paternal function intact are more destructive to women than boys matured through fathers. Boys *will* take. Fathers control that taking. Remove fathers, boys will take uncontrollably. When boys take uncontrollably, what is destroyed? Society. Who gets most hurt? Women.

It's the same story over and over again. And it always will be. Just look at the age-old tale of Romeo and Juliet. Before Shakespeare brought it to life and to its nearly perfect form, it existed in some version or other at least as far back as the Greco-Roman period, nearly two thousand years ago, perhaps, even before that. What's more important, however, is that this "mythology" attracts us even today. Why? What's going on in this apparently simple portrayal of young love thwarted by familial strife? The answer is not too difficult to understand in light of our explorations so far: The woeful story of Juliet and her Romeo epitomizes the explosive ambivalence of youthful male sexuality which can, if not controlled by the paternal function, just as easily find expression in the overwhelming passion of our "star-crossed" lovers as it does in the senseless slaughter of Mercutio, Tybalt, Paris, and a multitude of Capulets and Montagues, as well as the subsequent suicides of Romeo and Juliet, children sacrificed to a childish idealization of "amour." What excites and moves us about this tale, however, is its epiphany, which forces us to confront the destructive nature of unbridled adolescent masculine passion in conflict with society and the love of a woman: The drama is "exciting," for it brings to light the inevitable tragedy of unrestricted immature masculinity; ironically, in uncontrolled male energy, there is an unlimited potential for great sexual pleasure and, simultaneously, an equally great potential for enormous pain and destruction.

In "fair Verona," where "we lay our scene," the young males, the Capulets and the Montagues, are unchecked in their masculine desires. Their passions are given free reign by the immaturity of their feuding patriarchs, the effeminate unconditional acceptance of the "well intentioned" Friar Lawrence, and the "winking" eye of their less than patriarchal monarch. Consequently, out of the unsupervised adolescence of these teenaged boys arises the equally consuming forces of love and hate – all in one. So what begins as a "bawdy" comedy encircling the torrid passion of our young lovers ends in a tragedy where "all are punished," a tragedy unfortunately not only confined to the ancient streets of fair

Verona or the story of a more modern inner city's "west side," but also one played out in the narrow, overcrowded halls of each and every one of our school buildings, where today boys and girls raised without fathers "brush shoulders" and lock eyes in equally ambivalent acts of potentially consuming passion and anger.

VIII

Actually, there's an intriguing little bit more to the picture, so allow me to go off on yet another tangent before we get back to the importance of the father/son relationship. As "guarantors of the law," fathers have an additional function. This one revolves around incest and the mother/son relationship. It is the paternal function that must wean his children, sons and daughters alike, from what the father perceives to be the mother's suffocating, unconditional love. But, when it comes to sons, however, the father's law has another component; it is the father's function to come between his wife and her sons to – in that way – turn them from their mother and make them suitable lovers and, ultimately, satisfactory mates for women outside the family circle. Without this facet of the paternal function, boys may come to Oedipal tragedy and fall victim to the unhealthy ravages of classical mother/whore complexes. What do I mean? Let me explain.

It has been my contention, all along here, that contemporary America is suffering from its rejection and denigration of the paternal function, so, if I am correct, we should see evidence of this "mother/whore" dilemma, where men cannot deal with both aspects of femininity in the same woman, because it is a major symptom of father loss. And do we! Have you ever listened to the lyrics of a "rap" song? Ever hear of date rape and gang rape? How many young girls are being forced to do "things" they don't want to do by boys who don't believe no means "no"? How many women are complaining because they are unable to find men who are willing to "commit"? All of these are evidence of the severity of the immaturity of American males, caught in the Oedipal mother/whore tragedy. In "rap," women are "ho's," that means whores. Why? Because, to the immature male, there are only two types of women: mothers and whores. A male can only have one biological mother; even the number of women a man can call "mom" is limited. So, after these "mother women" are eliminated, all other women have to be whores. But why is this male's perspective so perverted and extreme? There is a reciprocity, more of a "catch 22," in the unconditional love a mother gives. Remember, maturation is a process of severing one's *self* from mother – first physically then symbolically. When a boy cannot mature, that is, when he cannot separate from his mother, he loses his male identity. If he does not have his male identity, he cannot enter into a commitment with a woman other than mom. He is absorbed into *her* identity. They are "as one." Just ask any woman who's been frustrated in her attempts to come between one of these boys and his mother! Whose side does he take? And, from the mother's perspective, any woman who comes between her and her identification with her son is an evil usurper. Nevertheless, despite the mother's great desire, a mother's influence isn't always total. There is a "fly" in the ointment, her son's fly, that is.

What "edge" does an "invading" woman have over the mother's hold on her boy? Sex! And, as we all know, sex is a powerful edge to have. So how does the mother keep this "sexy" woman from taking her son? She denigrates the woman by, ironically, reducing her, totally, to that sexual identity. She becomes a woman *only* good for sex, nothing else. Consequently, her son can have sex with that "other woman," but he can never relate to her or enter into a relationship with her, so his mother can never really lose him, for – more likely than not – the mother/son relationship would never become sexual anyway, so the minute he's done, he'll come running back to "mom." Therefore, she can let him "do" with this other woman, this whore, whatever he likes; her sexuality cannot come between mother and son. Because mother and son have *identified*, her perspective is his perspective. Hence, except for his mom, of course, all women are whores because they are only good for sex and are, therefore, unworthy of forming a relationship with him. Ironically, for many of these men, sex isn't even the object of their desire; denigration is. Do you see why? They have to denigrate the women with whom they have sex, so they are not obligated to respect them and, subsequently, are not forced to form a relationship with them which would be "unfaithful" to his relationship with mother. Ultimately, then, they have to either denigrate women or enter into sado-masochistic relationships that, at once, satisfy the pleasure principle while at the same time provide the punishment for abandoning "mother."

The paternal function is practically all that stands between boys and the tragic delusions of an Oedipal mother/whore complex. Fathers separate sons from mothers. Fathers turn boys away, so they can develop relationships with women outside the family. Furthermore, fathers teach boys to respect women, all women: mothers, daughters, sisters, wives. And, perhaps even more importantly, fathers teach daughters to respect themselves, so they don't fall prey to the immaturity of "taking" males as well as to denigration by Oedipally afflicted sons. From the boy's perspective, if the girl is "giving it away" so easily and freely, it cannot have much value to her, so why should he be expected to value it or, more importantly, to value her? Here's a story for you: One of my female students was crying in my office. We were going over a research paper, and she just started crying. Of course, I asked what was the matter. It seemed, she had just been rejected by the young man she thought was her "boyfriend." When I inquired about their relationship, their "commitment," she replied, "It's not like that anymore. It's different than it was in *your* day. Boys don't ask you out for dates. You just, sort of, 'hang out' together." She could tell I didn't understand. "Look," she continued, almost in frustration. "We were at a party, a bunch of us, and I got stoned and, well, somehow I was in some bed, and he was there too. It just happened." I was astonished. "You mean you didn't even know him before that," I asked. "*Who* was in the bed with you didn't matter?" You can guess the answer.

But we'll come to the father/daughter relationship shortly. For now, a few more thoughts on the mother/whore complex that is a product of father loss before returning to the process of father/son identification.

Without fathers, boys have great difficulty learning to respect women. Left to their own devices, young males develop little to no sense of an *equality* between the genders. The immaturity of their selfish taking nature causes them to believe there is an inferiority to giving and, consequently, to those who give. If they are hunters, immature males rationalize, than women are prey. And hunters, they believe, are far superior to their prey. Therefore, men are superior to women. Pretend you are the proverbial "fly" on the wall, this time in a boys' locker room. I don't think what you'll discover there about adolescent male attitudes towards women (girls) is going to surprise you. To the immature and inexperienced young male, what girls *do* sexually and, therefore by extension, what girls *are*, proves they are inferior to males. For example, the most effective way one immature male can denigrate another is to cast him into female roles, especially relating to the sex act: "suck this," "sit on this," "jerk this," "fuck you" – I'm sure I don't have to continue – are all effective "put downs," if not "fighting words," to immature males. The point is the boy is led to believe that anything females do, especially what females do during the sex act, is degrading. Imagine the confusion our young male experiences when his first girlfriend becomes sexually active with him. He's "mad" about her, but what kind of person would do what she's doing – and like it! Remember his locker room conditioning? Consequently, to many boys, the sex act is really an exercise in degrading women and, thereby, proving that males are superior. Isn't that what rape is all about? Sexual pleasure is secondary to a rapist's desire to degrade and "punish" his victim for having an inferior female sexual identity which, ironically, his great masculinity cannot control.

Controlling feminine sexuality is, in fact, "the" great burden for immature males as illustrated by Shakespeare's Othello who, growing ever more and more insanely jealous over what he believes to be his bride Desdemona's sexual promiscuity, vents in a soliloquy his confusion and frustration, "O curse of marriage!/That we can call these delicate creatures ours,/And not their appetites! I had rather be a toad/And live upon the vapor of a dungeon/Than keep a corner in the thing I love for others' uses" (III, iii). His inability to control her sexuality is, in fact, what ultimately brings him to "put out her light," to kill her, before "she'll betray more men." As he approaches her bed, driven by jealousy to strangle her to death with his bare hands, the light he carries, flickering before his eyes in the darkened room, illuminates her great beauty forcing him to cry out in an ambivalence of emotive chaos born of the incongruous "marriage" of attraction and repulsion, "It is the cause, it is the cause, my soul./Let me not name it to you, you chaste stars,/It is the cause" (V, ii). "It," that is, the "cause," is Desdemona's beauty, her desirability, her attraction, yet "it" is also the feminine "mystique" that no man can resist, let alone understand or ever hope to control. Nevertheless, the immature male keeps trying to control women, usually through the processes of reducing them or dehumanizing them. Think of how many "animal" names men have for women: "chick," "fox," "bird" or even the more derogatory terms "old hen," "crow," "cow," and "bitch." And, too, aren't the best of them, the so-called "pet" names, really a way of dehumanizing women – just like "pudding" "tomato," and "honey," which turns females into foods? What about "baby" or "doll"? Isn't that a way to reduce women too? More obvious is the male reduction of women to sexual body parts. How many names do men have for female sex organs? Be honest, how many "names" can you think of for breasts, for asses, let alone anything else. Why do men do this? To control feminine sexuality, of course. But does it work?

Think about it. Let's go back to our young locker room boy's horror and confusion when he first falls in love, and the "divine creature" he is "mad about" begins to perform all those "degrading" things he's heard about from that locker room and, worse, she is enjoying doing so? She *wants* to do them! And she finds other men attractive and would do these degrading things with other men! He is traumatized. How does he separate the pleasures of her "magical" feminine sexuality he is enjoying from her demeaning, whorish "slutty" behavior? How can he still respect her? How can he even continue to love her? She is a debased creature who does unthinkable things – unthinkable, at least, to his immature perspective of sexuality. Of course, there's no problem if he can simply enjoy her "favors" then leave. Let some other guy deal with her whorishness. And that is the solution for many immature males: "Find 'em, feel 'em, fuck 'em, and forget 'em." But, if he loves her, how does he deal with leaving her? He cannot. His only answer, the only way he can make sense of the whole situation, is to make sure she does this with no one else but him. All right, he rationalizes, she does degrading things, but she does them *to* him, *for* him. Her "demeaning" acts are a "special" activity reserved for him and him alone. He can understand the things she lets him do *to* her and the things she does *for* him by making himself believe she allows herself to be debased because she loves *him*. He has no idea they are "equal" partners in love-making or anything else, for that matter. What she does sexually, though of great pleasure to him, is nevertheless "disgusting" and "repulsive." He can't even think of doing any of these things. Consequently, if she displays any hint of sexuality independent of their love-making or is attracted to any other male, all his "excuses" for her indefensible behavior evaporate, and she is a "whore." The only way he can accept her sexuality is if he believes she has no sexuality – except for *him*. She does all these self-degrading things for *him* because she loves *him* and is willing to debase herself to make *him* happy. Therefore, her "servicing" him sexually is her sacrifice of her dignity to him. The pressure on her to maintain his "fantasy" is enormous. She constantly walks a fine line, behaviorally. The slightest provocation or even the suspicion that there's another man and he can become, like Othello, obsessively jealous, angry, even physically abusive. With an immature male, a woman is always in danger of being denigrated, hurt, and abandoned as "worthless."

These boys could drive a woman insane – just ask, for instance, Shakespeare's Ophelia, torn between a father's influence and a lover's Oedipal ambivalence. Though warned repeatedly (and, perhaps, insensitively) by her father Polonius and her brother Laertes about the selfish sexual motivations of young men like Hamlet, Ophelia – despite the loss of her self-worth contributed to her father and brother's feeble mechanizations to control her sexuality by telling her she is not worthy of such a match with the heir apparent – cannot help but love the prince who has been aggressively wooing her, for she has no way of knowing how deep-rooted is Hamlet's Oedipal crisis. First, Hamlet cannot deal with his mother's sexuality. He perceives her as an "unweeded garden,/that grows to seed." Worse, he blames the weakness of his father for allowing her wild feminine nature to go unchecked. His father was too "nice" and, "so loving to my mother,/That he might not beteem the winds of heaven/Visit her face too roughly." From Hamlet's perspective, a woman cannot help being attractive. It is her "nature." Consequently, her sexuality is out of control, for she has no desire to curb that which makes her so visible. Thus, she is subject to the possession of any man, no matter how gross in nature, as long as he displays the appropriate male response, powerful aggression – that is, "taking." Besides, she cannot selectively lure one man to her; rather, she is a torch that draws every male moth, no matter how unsavory, to its flame. Thus, she is prone to indiscriminately giving herself to the sexual advances of the greatest of kings as well as the lustiest of Satyrs – as long as they are willing to possess her aggressively. Or so thinks Hamlet, anyway. This is why Hamlet concludes his analogy about his mother's "unweeded" sexuality with his Oedipal complaint that, "things rank and gross in nature/Possess it merely." At once, he blames his father for not controlling his mother's sexuality and his mother for being, by nature, an uncontrollable sex object. "Frailty, thy name is woman!"

Second, enter Ophelia – How does Hamlet's Oedipal dilemma impact their relationship? If Hamlet is correct, she too must be a "garden," forever watched over and "weeded," for she too is a woman and one whose sexuality is just coming to bloom. This is why her father and her brother are forever pruning and "cutting her back," by warning her of Hamlet's sexual, not marital, desires:

> *For lord Hamlet,*
> *Believe so much in him, that he is young;*
> *And with a larger tether may he walk,*
> *Than may be given you: in few, Ophelia,*
> *Do not believe his vows; for they are brokers;*
> *Not of that dye which their investments show,*
> *But mere implorators of unholy suits,*
> *Breathing like sanctified and pious bonds,*
> *The better to beguile.*
> (I, iii)

Is Polonius being insensitive to his daughter's rights by inflicting this seemingly "double standard" on her, or is he merely trying to fulfill his paternal function, to allow his daughter to wake up to the necessity of her curbing her "natural" inclination to indiscriminate "giving"? Succinctly, are we "turned off" by his pomposity or by his message? He is definitely a pedant, but it is not the man who is important; it is the paternal function. And, if we think about it honestly, what he is doing is quite beneficial for Ophelia. By giving her the "truth" about young men in general, he is empowering her to make more informed decisions and, thereby, take control of her own life. If he doesn't, then – as Hamlet believes – it is her husband's role to control her, to keep her "weeded." Without the paternal function, she is at the mercy of the first man who can aggressively possess her. What Polonius fears is that some man will enter his daughter's garden, deposit his seed, and leave her in a mess. Think about it, if she had entered quickly into a sexual relationship with Hamlet, would he respect her or wish to marry her? Probably not. Thus, the paternal function, as restricting as it may be, is not meant to hurt the daughter; its purpose is to provide her with a masculine perspective which, if she is wise, she can add to her feminine emotive strengths. The paternal function does not dictate the daughter be asexual. All it's saying is be discriminate when you *do* give yourself. Make sure, when you give yourself, the man values your gift and is willing to give to you in return, especially in terms of a commitment to a relationship.

Unfortunately, as expected, Hamlet's Oedipal behavior more than proves Polonius correct. Understandably so, Ophelia, with the admonishments of her father and brother ringing in her ears, feels the need to "test" Hamlet. She, like every woman before and after her, needs to know if he is the genuine article or just some lusty and selfish fellow. Indeed, the medieval age of "courtly love" was almost comically overwhelmed with knights trying to prove their mettle and sincerity of love to their ladies. Testing was then, as it is now, a major portion of the wooing process. This is why Ophelia returns Hamlet's "gifts." If we believe this "special" young lady is simply following her father's orders like an automaton, then we do not know the hearts of young ladies at all. For Ophelia, returning Hamlet's gifts is a way to accomplish both goals: She can obey her father *and* test Hamlet's love at the same time. Thus, when she hands her prince the "remembrances," she informs him that she had "longed long to re-deliver" them. What is the inference? The inference is that he has been taking too long with the commitment portion of his love-making. Gift giving has been a way to keep her "hanging on" without really making any commitment. But there's more, for she is also saying that she has waited a long time to bring this moment to its "head" and that she has longed for this moment of "truth," to see if he truly loves her. Hamlet fails miserably. He denies ever giving her the "remembrances," to which denial she responds, "you know right well you did;/And, with them, words of so sweet breath compos'd/As made the things more rich: their perfume lost,/Take these again; for to the noble mind/Rich gifts wax poor when givers prove unkind." She ends with the short exclamation, "There, my lord," which, at once, is a return of his "remembrances" and an invisible slap in the face, a "take that."

Hamlet is no fool, however. Remember, he is only pretending to be insane. He knows she loves him. This is not his problem. His problem is that he cannot value the love of a woman because he believes that women give love too freely and that men, including himself, take advantage of "giving" women and, thereby, cheapen the women and their gifts:

Get thee to a nunnery; why wouldst thou
be a breeder of sinners? I am myself indifferent

honest; but yet I could accuse me of such things,
that it were better my mother had not borne
me: I am very proud, revengeful, ambitious, with
more offenses at my beck than I have thoughts
to put them in, imagination to give them shape, or
time to act them in. What should fellows as
I do crawling between heaven and earth! We are
arrant knaves, all; believe none of us. Go thy
ways to a nunnery. Where's your father?
(III, i)

Hamlet's final question could be his recognition that her father put her up to this or, just as easily, that her father should have been better "weeding" his daughter's wild garden, for Hamlet knows that Ophelia would give herself to him if he gave her the slightest hint of reciprocal love. And this thought is what drives him insane, that women give themselves to men who don't appreciate them – even him. From Hamlet's Oedipal perspective, the woman he loves should be forever chaste and free from the degradation of male sexual desires – somehow, ironically, even his own. He does not see the sex act as a mutual expression of love. In his "locker room" mentality, sex is how men degrade women. From an adolescent male perspective, women perform degrading acts during sex. So where's the "rub"? Hamlet, like "everyman," cannot help but love these women. It is this love/hate ambivalence that drives him crazy, the idea that the same woman one man "degrades" sexually becomes another man's "mother" – especially his mother – is "maddening." Hamlet cannot come to grips with his idea that in "marriage" a man is made to accept both aspects of femininity, both faces, the mother and the whore:

I have heard of your paintings too, well
enough; God hath given you one face, and you
make yourselves another: you jig, you amble, and
you lisp, and nick-name God's creatures, and make
your wantonness your ignorance. Go to, I'll no
more on it; it hath made me mad. I say, we
will have no more marriages; those that are mar-
ried already – all but one – shall live; the rest

shall keep as they are. To a nunnery, go.
(III, i)

Before you dismiss the Oedipal illness of our young Prince of Denmark as an aberration, a literary abstraction, remember this: What gives Shakespeare's play its energy is its mythopoeic nature. There were many Hamlets before Shakespeare's immortal recreation. Hamlet and Ophelia are not simply words on a sheet of paper; they are archetypes of young men and women from the beginning of recorded time to the present moment. Hamlet's Oedipal ambivalence is the same crisis today's immature males confront: How do they separate mothers from whores? Or, worse, how can they accept women who proudly boast of being both? Today, there are Hamlets everywhere and even more wounded Ophelias. For example, one of my neighbors is a young girl about fifteen years of age. She recently began "dating" an older boy, old enough to drive, perhaps, seventeen. For about three or four months, they were inseparable. Everyday after school, he would pick her up, and they would – tires squealing – drive off, her hanging onto his neck like a scarf, into the proverbial "sunset." She was "all smiles" for awhile. Then, suddenly, he was gone. He began dating her "best friend," as a matter of fact, the one to whom she introduced him. Now, she is devastated. She is visibly hurt and mourning deeply. It's actually painful just to see her. Her parents are worried. She cries at the cliched "drop of a hat," neglects her studies, and has no appetite. She *is* Ophelia. Shakespeare's Ophelia sings of being "loaded all with sweet flowers," to the grave and, in her insanity, gives away imaginary columbines, fennels, daisies, and violets, the very "gifts" of her "secret" garden. She sings too of her betrayal, "Young men will do it, if they come to 't;/By cock they are to blame./Quoth she, before you tumbled me,/You promis'd me to wed." And, adorned with flowered garlands, she meets her death drowned while trying to pick the phallic, "long purples/That liberal shepherds give a grosser name,/But our cold maids do dead men's fingers call them," giving her flowered self to "muddy death." My young female neighbor, feeling the emptiness of her deflowering, drowns herself too – not in muddy death – rather, in the waters of the unconscious, in despair. In contrast, "he" is merrily on his way, on to the next "conquest." They had sex, of course, but to him it meant "nothing." It all happened in *her* body. He was just a "visitor." She wasn't discriminate about his entrance, why should he be? Therefore, and, more importantly to him, why should he care about his exit? If she didn't want to, she shouldn't have. He didn't force her. She should have known better. It takes "two to tango," so what's all the fuss about? Anyway, she's just a girl. What did she expect? He's the "man." And that's what men do.

Where's poppa? This boy needs a father! It is the paternal function to teach him the "truth" about women and about how real men behave. Now, don't confuse the contemporary Hollywood notion that real men are those who go through women two and three at a time. And don't confuse real men with these so-called athletes who boast of having hundreds and hundreds of women. They are not real men. They are not fathers. The father must teach his son that *different* things can be *equal*, that men and women, though they *are* different, are nevertheless equal. In fact, I believe this was the function of the rituals held all those tens of thousands of millennia ago in prehistoric caves. Young boys were brought to those caves, not to learn how to hunt; learning how to hunt was better carried out in the external world above the caves. In the darkness of the caves, which symbolized the male womb as much as it did the womb of mother earth, the boys were symbolically "born again" as mature males, whose epiphany was an awakening to the "truth" that hunter and prey were equal partners in a mutually satisfying symbiotic relationship. The maturing of these boys as hunters was their realization that hunter and prey were *different* but *equal*. Our prehistoric ancestors did not believe they were superior to the animals. They saw themselves in competition with them. They recognized and valued the different strengths and qualities of each animal. They learned respect for the predators and the prey and, therefore, respect for all other things that may be different – most importantly, they learned respect for women. The boy learned how to properly utilize his "natural" gift, his strength (whatever it may be), and that his strength was not to be misused. He hunted to supply his tribe with food, not to wantonly destroy his quarry in a show of his superiority. When he went to battle, he did so to protect his tribe, not to inflict senseless pain. His warring and his hunting were his service to "life," that is, to the women who gave birth to and nurtured, with the very milk of their breasts, "life."

Consequently, the paternal function is *not* about male selfishness and male dominance as those who oppose it wish us to believe. Much to their dismay, the paternal function proves to be, ultimately, as self-sacrificial as maternity. But where are our fathers? We need them now, more than ever.

IX

Contemporary America suffers greatly from the emasculation of the paternal function. In today's so-called "civilized" societies, most of the maturation rituals are either lost or so reduced they are barely recognizable, let alone effective. For example, what's the original meaning of the Hebrew circumcision rite? Does the current practice, performed so soon after the birth of a baby boy, have anything to do now with male maturation? It probably did some long time ago. I can't believe it originated simply to recognize the boy child as a member of the tribe. Even the *Bar Mitzvah* is a shadow of what it once must have been. There is very little recognition of a male maturation rite, especially now that there is an ever growing impetus to include women in the form of the *Bas Mitzvah*. What about the Christian concept of Baptism? Do we perceive it now as a second birth, a symbolic rebirth, through the father? And Confirmation! The young initiates, males and females alike, get a gentle slap on the side of the face. It has been reduced that much. The ritual has lost almost all of its maturation functioning.

Because these rituals are no longer potent concrete experiences, children – especially young males – are forced to endure their suffering nowadays on a psychological rather than a physiological level. The inability of males to mature in contemporary America is a failed physical process that has become riddled, subsequently, with psychic scarifications: love/hate ambivalence and its resultant dependency; loss of identity; guilt; and the anxiety and violence that stem from the emotive Oedipal confusion. We are all familiar with the "Oedipus Complex," yet, contrary to popular conception, the male child's love of his mother is *not* the origin of guilt and anxiety. Rather, it is the boy's ambivalent feelings towards his father that are the cause of most neuroses. As Freud argues in *Totem and Taboo*, it is this ambivalence inherent in the father/son relationship that is, in fact, central not only to the individual's development of guilt and anxiety, but also to the development of guilt and anxiety in society, itself.

At about the same time the boy is developing a love relationship with his mother, he is also developing a unique relationship with his father. Male children "identify" with their fathers. Sons begin to demonstrate a "special" interest in their fathers. They want to grow up "just like daddy" and take his place everywhere. "A little boy will exhibit a special interest in his father; he would like to grow up like him and be like him, and take his place everywhere. We may say simply that he takes his father as his ideal" (Freud, "Group Psych," 105). The father becomes an ideal, a *function*, which the boy seeks to assume. As can be readily inferred, this "identification" is ambivalent from the beginning. The boy not only loves his father, but also wants to take his father's place. Freud continues, "Identification, in fact, is ambivalent from the very first; it can turn into an expression of tenderness as easily as into a wish for someone's removal" (105). This ambivalence in the process of identification is evident from the earliest onset of the Oedipal dilemma. It can be expressed in a loving, tender way or, just as easily, as the desire to usurp the father's power and authority – if not his life.

This ambivalence, ironically, is what keeps the Oedipal sons in check. They want to overtake the father, but they also love the father and admire him, so they don't want to lose him. They simultaneously need and fear his strength. Consequently, any act of aggression against the father would activate their guilt and create the anxiety that results from the loss of his love and the fear of reprisal from the bigger and stronger patriarch – a revenge that could result, the boy anticipates with dread – in castration (given the sexual motivation of the boy's Oedipal complex) or even death. Totally confused, the boy transfers his own love and hate onto the father. The son projects his ambivalent sexual and selfish motives and believes the father, too, simultaneously loves and hates; consequently, the boy "walks a thin line" between procuring the father's love and avoiding his vengeful wrath. So what's a boy to do? Is there a way out? Most importantly, what is worse, being caught in the Oedipal dilemma or having to endure the loss of the paternal function?

Without a doubt, father loss is by far the greater of the "two evils." To prove my point, let's return once more to the concept of boys joining gangs in this fatherless society of ours. Although no one today takes literally (or even seriously as an anthropological certainty) the "Primal Father" scenario that Sigmund Freud proposes in *Totem and Taboo*, it does serve mythologically to metaphorically illustrate that young males who band into gangs do so out of frustration, not choice, and are, consequently, dissatisfied, for joining a gang is a miserable "compromise." Gang membership is a recognition of the loss of independence and male maturity identification with the "Primal Father" promises. You cannot be a member of a "gang" and assume "Primal Father" ascendancy at the same time. Therefore, given the choice, boys would much rather seek maturity and all its rewards through paternal identification than endure membership in a gang and suffer the anonymous ignominy of immaturity. In fact, the "bottom line" in contemporary American society is young boys are *forced* to join gangs because of the paucity of mature males with whom they can identify. If there were real fathers, there would be no gangs. Ultimately, gang membership, despite any superficial reward, can satisfy only secondary wish fulfillments and not the primary desire to achieve the paternal identity. Consequently, young males are dissatisfied with gang membership because, as long as they are merely "members" of a gang, they cannot mature as individuals and inherit the role of "Primal Father."

Who is this Freudian "Primal Father," and what is his significance? Succinctly, and rather simplistically explained here, Freud asserts that, at some point in human history, there was a "Primal Father," a dominant male. This Primal Father had total authority and possessed all the goods, all the power, and all the females. His reign was not untroubled though, for, over time, the Primal Father would have sired a great number of children, some male and some female. The females he would simply keep for himself, forever increasing the size of his harem. However, the males – his sons – were a different story. The inexorable processes of time were against him: As his sons grew older and stronger, he was simultaneously growing older and weaker; consequently, he was in constant danger of one of them eventually opposing him and usurping his "throne." Thus, his only means of survival was to rid himself of these ever threatening sons, so he either killed them or banished them far away from his sight. Out of necessity, these "exiled" sons banded together to survive. They formed a "band" or "gang," but such membership was a compromise to each individual son. More importantly, as each reached puberty, each desired to possess some, if not all, of the father's women and, more importantly, the patriarchal authority itself. But this "wish fulfillment" was still very nearly a "hopeless case" because each of these sons was still quite immature, and the father was still much too big and strong, so there was no way any one son could actually defeat the father and usurp the paternal role. In fact, to even try would result in death or castration. Therefore, the boys could only overthrow their father if they attacked him – all together – in a group.

According to Freud, this "brother band" did just that. *En masse*, they eventually succeeded in opposing and defeating the father. Furthermore, they slew him and ate him in an horrific yet ultimate expression of "communal communion" and, quite literally, father "identification." By consuming the flesh of the father, they hoped to physically possess his strength, majesty, and, most importantly, his "identity" – "You are what you eat." This is, in fact, the idea behind cannibalism. For the most part, cannibals will not consume an inferior human being, for that would fill them with that person's inferiority; rather, their desire is to eat their most revered ancestors or their most powerful enemies to, in that way, assimilate their strength and wisdom. Nevertheless, perhaps without realizing, this brother band "meal," this consuming of the patriarch, was also essential food for the brothers' troubled psyches. Victory was *bitter*sweet: The father was loved and esteemed as well as jealously hated. After all, the father fed and protected them through the dependency of their prepubescent years enabling them, ironically, to grow to usurp his power. Therefore, despite their joy of victory, from the guilty and frustrated perspective of these sons, the father's overthrow was a traitorous act, perpetrated by this "brother band" against the father who helped give them life and whose stature could never be attained by any of them. Together these "lesser" boys defeated a paternal giant, whose regal status none of them could ever hope to even approach. Indeed, the victory was more than bittersweet. It was downright sour: Because of the gang's "covenant," no *one* son could claim all the women or hope to possess the dead father's power for himself. In truth, no one son actually "earned" the patriarchal role. Instead, all of the sons had to compromise or abandon their "Primal Father" desires to avoid the fate of their slain patriarch, for the "brother band" would destroy any one male who tried, from then on, to install himself as the new "Primal Father."

In this way, the potentialities and rewards of individualism and risk gave way to the frustrating mediocrity of gang membership and the ultimate loss of the son's maturity and potential to assume the Primal Father identity. Thus, the mythological age of "giants" came to an abrupt and unsatisfactory end for these disillusioned brothers, replaced forevermore by an unattainable paternal signifier, "the *name* of the Father." This "age of giants" giving way to a current race of "inferior" gods is a common mythological motif. The Greek gods defeated the Titans. And, in Scandinavia, *Ragnarok* is the battle that results in the mutual destruction of all the warring gods and giants. The battle is inevitable.

Consequently, we cannot really blame Freud's brother band patricides, for, you see, Oedipal ambivalence makes it impossible for sons to discern the paternal function until after the father's death, so the father's death – as cruel as it may seem – is essential. As long as the father presides, the son's response is confusion; he both loves and hates the father who protects him yet "blocks" – as the boy sees it – his path to maturity. Thus, the father must be destroyed, but only the father, not his function. In his brilliant modern day Oedipal "mythology," *The Dead Father*, Donald Barthelme gives colorful voice to the immature son's "father" frustration:

Fathers are like blocks of marble, giant cubes, highly
polished, with veins and seams, placed squarely in your
path. They block your path. They cannot be climbed
over, neither can they be slithered past. They are the
"past,"and very likely the slither, if the slither is
thought of as that accommodating maneuver you make to
escape notice, or get by unscathed. If you attempt to
go around one, you will find that another (winking at
the first) has mysteriously appeared athwart the trail.
Or maybe it is the same one, moving with the speed of
paternity.
(280)

As the above so creatively illustrates, the wish for the father's removal is an integral part of the Oedipal complex. Yet, as we can see, inherent in that wish is the removal of *only* the physical father. It is the father, whom he perceives as a barrier between him and his Oedipal desires, that the boy wishes to remove – *not* the paternal function. He wants to maintain ownership of the paternal function for himself. Tragically, however, the question of the father in contemporary America is essentially one of *total paternal absence* – not just the absence of the father, the absence of the paternal function itself – an unsatisfactory, compromised condition quite reminiscent of the dilemma Freud's "brother band" conspirators faced after their rash rebellion.

Under the auspices of the "Primal Father," when the physical source of Oedipal ambivalence, the physical father, is removed, the essential, symbolic maturation process is not. In fact, it is intensified, for only after the father is lost can the son come to realize the *function* of paternity, and it is the function that is important, not the individual father. Unfortunately, though, the paternal function, itself, has now been lost – just as it was in Freud's "Primal Father" narrative – so young males today, like their brother band counterparts, have neither the father nor his function. Without fathers, they've lost it all. Consequently, by extension, the compromise of brother band membership metaphorically illustrates the frustration, guilt and anxiety gang mentality causes for young males today.

So why *do* they join gangs? And how did all this happen? How did we lose the paternal function? Was Freud right? Did sons, unthinkingly and selfishly, band together to destroy the father only to discover, after their rash and brutal act, how much they loved the father and how much each individual son lost when he surrendered his birthright, the paternal function, to a group mentality?

Before we can answer these questions, we need to thoroughly explore the absence of the father and, subsequently, the great importance of the paternal function to males because what I wish to prove is that – contrary to Freud's "Primal Father" theory – sons are *not* responsible for father absence, especially in America today. Sons need and want paternity. Sure, they may harbor Oedipal fantasies that have them defeating the father, but, as Freud's "Primal Father" narrative proves, that victory is, in the end, unacceptable, for it is compromised, at best. It is "soured," in fact, the moment the son realizes he cannot usurp the paternal function for himself. So, no, it was not the son – as a member of a brother band or otherwise – who rebelled against the father. And, just as importantly, it is not the son's Oedipal desire that is fueling contemporary America's anti-patriarchal hatred.

X

Recently, the most intriguing psychoanalytical understanding of the father, especially of the paternal function, emanates from the theories of Jacques Lacan. Admittedly hermetic, the "French Freud" redefines the paternal function in terms of, ironically, its absence. Quite simplistically stated here is a brief outline of my "sketchy" understanding of the basic ideas of Lacanian philosophy: First, the initial absolute subjectivity of the child allows his awareness of the "other" (that is, everything that is not actually the child, him- or herself) to manifest only after the other is removed from the child's belief in the "oneness" of self and "all"; only when the other is objectified, that is, externalized, realized as separate or missing from the self, can it or its function be perceived. Thus, for the other to be discovered by the child, it must first be removed – absent. Then, and only then, can its "otherness" make it recognizable. The child must first realize the other's absence from the subjectivity of self before he can recognize its objective existence. Hence, the function of the "other" is discovered by its absence from the self.

Second, more specifically in terms of the paternal function, the Lacanian concept of an "absent" father proves to be "symbolic." Anthony Wilden, translator of Lacan's *The Language of the Self*, explains, "What the subject must seek is what Lacan calls the symbolic identification with the father – that is to say, he must take over the *function* of the father through the normalization of the Oedipus complex. This is an identification with the father who is neither Imaginary nor real: what Lacan calls the Symbolic father, the figure of the Law" (165). Therefore, according to Lacan, the function of the father is to be "guarantor of the law." Basically, it is the father as "law" who comes between the mother and child to sever the psychic umbilical, establishing society and, subsequently, identity.

Initially, the child perceives the mother "as one" with its self; the mother is its complement, its primal object of desire. The mother's desire is also complementary, for she wishes her child to be the fulfillment of her own "lack," that is, to be the "phallus" to fill her void. Naturally, the child strives to satisfy her desire by *becoming* the phallus. In a normal relationship, however, the mother also accepts the father – as *possessor* of the phallus. Once the child recognizes this acceptance, the child necessarily abandons his fantasy of *becoming* the phallus to, instead, compete with the father for *possession* of the phallus. It is the father's function, therefore, to separate mother and child and, in the process, lay down the law and set the norms of his society. In this way, the child, doomed to lose the initial combat to his far more powerful foe, is weaned from the "oneness" of maternity to find the identity his place in society affords. In *The Lives and Legends of Jacques Lacan*, Catherine Clement asserts, "If...the mother recognizes in the father the function of establishing the rule of the law of societies by respecting his speech, then the child can accept symbolic castration by the father and by gaining access to the order of the symbol, he will find the original signifier of the self: the name and the place he is destined to occupy in the family constellation" (234).

Ultimately, then, to Lacan, the father is the Symbolic father, who, as guarantor of the Law, is the Dead Father or "pure signifier," that is, the "Name-of-the-Father." Wilden explains further, "The Symbolic father is not a real or an Imaginary father (imago), but corresponds to the mythical Symbolic father of *Totem and Taboo*. The requirements of Freud's theory, says Lacan, led him 'to link the opposition of the signifier of the Father, as author of the Law, to death, or rather to the murder of the Father, thus demonstrating that if this murder is the fruitful moment of the debt through which the subject binds himself for life to the law, the Symbolic father, in so far as he signifies that Law, is actually the Dead Father'" (270). The Dead Father is the distilled, pure essence of paternity, the "Name-of-the-Father," that is, the paternal function revealed by its absence.

This is all well and good to explain the normal Oedipal situation in societies where patriarchy is still intact and appreciated, but what I see in contemporary American culture is a purposely hurtful perversion of the traditional Oedipal son's dilemma. Nevertheless, when discussing the normal Oedipal drama, both Freud and Lacan recognize the son's wish to defeat the father and take his place, and both identify the love/hate ambivalence inherent in the son's inevitable victory. Freud's "Primal Father" parable and Lacan's philosophies also illustrate how the son only comes to realize the paternal function after the father's death. And these are great insights, but, in today's American society, these theories do not go far enough. They only deal with the difficulties and complexities of a transfer of power from father through paternal function to son, who becomes father and possessor of the paternal function only to be opposed in turn by his son, who usurps the paternal function, and so on. They do not take into consideration the tragedy we are now facing in America: the dissolution of the entire Oedipal father/son process. Now, in America, the father is lost and so is his function. There is no transfer of paternity from father to son. Everything has ended. But that's not all. In the traditional Oedipal conflict, the paternal function is always valued. The struggle to "possess the phallus" is always a worthwhile battle, for "to the winner go the spoils." Therefore, despite all the psychic baggage, sons actively seek the normalization of their Oedipal conflicts. But, now, all that is different. In American society, the paternal function has been discredited and denigrated, so much so, boys are actually turned away from identification with it.

Patriarchy has become a "four-letter word" in American society today. Everything "male" – another four-letter word – is hateful and ignorant. The paternal function has been so devalued, in fact, that it no longer has any worth whatsoever; consequently, it is now "lost" to young males, who – despite this severe societal loathing of mature patriarchy – still desperately need it. And so does the rest of society, including women. When fathers restrict their daughters' "giving" natures, they simultaneously control the destructive "taking" of males. Thus, the sexual restrictions imposed on females, under the traditional patriarchal system, is not a punitive measure; it is designed to protect the women from the uncontrolled masculine "urges" of immature males. Think about it. There is actually no other way to accomplish this end. Sexually aggressive males are nearly impossible to control. They would never deny themselves their pleasures. Consequently, without fathers, women are forced to keep these boys in check. That's why fathers try to teach their daughters about restricted giving – especially since these daughters are the vulnerable targets of uncontrolled male sexuality. Thus, the so-called "double standard" is not a punishment as some would have us believe. It is an effort to control nearly uncontrollable males by controlling the more malleable females who have the most influence over the boys – to the benefit of both! When male sexuality is controlled, females are protected from the destructive "machismo" that victimizes women. Males need the paternal function in place to assist them in their maturation processes and wean them from their "taking" natures, so they can return to these very same women to form mature relationships. And, best of all, a point that is very rarely made: When adolescent sexual activity is controlled, adolescence becomes a "magical" time of sexual fantasy and anticipation. For each gender, the "opposite sex" is an enticing and exciting "mystery," to be appreciated and enjoyed when one is mature enough to respect the sexual union and perceive copulation as a coming together of "equals," the satisfaction of the equation of life and love, $1 + 1 = 1$.

Conversely, without fathers, sex is anything but "special" and has very little to do with love, becoming instead a means of finding one's masculine identity in a string of "conquests" that dehumanizes women and refashions them as worthless "notches on a sexual gun." And what's worse is that women are now acting the same way, perhaps believing that the "only way to beat them is to join them." Sadly and tragically, young women are also trying to find their femininity in terms of sexual conquests. Consequently, today, sex is the everyday activity of children who, by the time they actually reach maturity, are "burned out" and, instead of developing a respect for the "mystery" of the opposite gender, hate the opposite sex so much they often act out in violence – to themselves and others. Perhaps, this is why so much of contemporary Hollywood sexuality is combined with violence. What is really being acted out on the sexual silver screen is anger!

It's actually painful to think of how little sex has to do with love these days. Romantic love and the idea that it matters "who's on top" have been sacrificed to impersonal sexuality that's almost a shared act of masturbation. How satisfying can sex be when, in the most "heated" moments, the partners – because most of the time they are nearly strangers – aren't even thinking of each other but are lost instead in moments of individual fantasy? Where's "love" when the couple are kissing and hugging outwardly while inwardly their minds are a proverbial "million miles away"? This loss of romantic love and its resultant cavalier attitude towards casual sex is what the absence of the paternal function has wrought upon our children, especially our daughters, for they are the ones who get hurt the most. Remember my young female student, crying over her lost "love."

What upset her, she continued, was that they had made love in the dark, and – all the while it was happening – she kept trying to remember what he looked like, but couldn't. Sadly, she's confused the idea of a relationship with the physical sex act itself. Obviously, her sexuality has nothing to do with love. It has all to do with having sex with some "faceless" someone who just happens to be there when she is in the mood. She thinks love will follow that sex act. She's wrong. And she's hurting. If she had a father, he would tell her, "love first – marriage next – then sex." But, in contemporary fatherless America, saying such a thing is considered chauvinistic and insensitive to women. The quick response is, "She has a right to do whatever she wants with her body." Well, she may have that right, but she needs guidance. Would you let a child put his or her finger in the electric socket because that child has a right to do whatever he or she wants with his or her body? Of course not. You would, as a parent, stop that child. Yet, as a parent, why are you reluctant to stop my young female student from having sex simply because she's in the mood, and there's an attractive male available? Does your responsibility as a parent end when the child reaches some arbitrary "legal" age limit? Is that it? Or are you afraid to stand up to the relativists, who tell us there are no "rights and wrongs," who say we should not be judgmental? As a parent – as a mother, as a father – you had better be prepared to tell your children what's right and what's wrong and, most importantly, why it's better for them to do what's right. And don't be afraid. You are not harming your children by "drawing lines in the sand." You are guiding them. The paternal function is to guide, not enslave. When someone asks, "Who is to judge," answer, "I am!" For heaven's sake listen to Mandela: You're playing small doesn't serve the world. Who are we to judge? We are manifestations of the glory of God

Young people seek guidance. They want to know where the boundary lines are. This doesn't mean they will observe those demarcations, for one of the functions of youth is to challenge authority and its dicta. But laws give them some sense of order, some sense of security and societal support. When we become relativists, we deny our children the guidance and structure they need to, ironically, go beyond our boundaries. Here's a cliched image: a toddler first learning to walk holding onto one parent's hand for security while reaching out, at the same time, to the other parent a few steps away. That's the idea! When we give our children rules and a definite belief system, we are not entrapping them – as relativists would have us believe – rather, we are providing them with a hand to hold onto as they build the courage and strength to let go and walk on their own.

As contemporary American culture illustrates, our children have been robbed of this parental, more specifically, paternal function. And this theft is especially damaging to the maturation of young males. Today, in America, each individual son is in tragic competition with not only an absent father but also an *absent* paternal function – tragic because the combat presents a "no win" situation. The individual cannot exist without this function; identity cannot be recognized without acceptance of the "other" and, subsequently, societal law. Consequently, in today's fatherless America, sons once torn by the normal processes of Oedipal love/hate ambivalence have, ironically, gotten their wish to witness the death of their fathers only to discover they must now combat the absent *function* of paternity in a war they cannot win. The father has been destroyed, but so has his paternal function to be guarantor of the law. Consequently, what contemporary American culture reveals is Oedipal entrapment and frustration. Fathers have given way, only to be replaced by metaphorical representations that are themselves now lost. Without fathers, sons can only rebel against paternal law, the "symbolic" father, but now that too is gone; consequently, they are forced to exist in narcissistic environs removed from culture and outside family. They suffer membership in nothing – except unsatisfactory "brother band" gangs. They are alienated, remote. Nothing they see is theirs. They experience no pride of ownership, no sense of responsibility. Look at our once great cities – they're destroyed. Try to find a public space or even a subway car that isn't now covered over with graffiti. They are being destroyed by young people who feel no sense of "ownership," no sense of inheritance. So they value nothing and destroy all that may unfortunately cross their path – be they cities or human beings.

Yes, the father has been defeated, but the son has not been victorious because the paternal function that was to be left behind has also been defeated. Consequently, father loss in America is obviously not the result of rebellious Oedipal sons, for they would have the father dead but the function intact. Therefore, something or someone else has purposely and utterly obliterated the paternal function. But who? And to what gain?

XI

Perhaps, the time has come to explore the relationship of the father with his "other" child, his daughter. The father/daughter relationship is so physiologically, psychologically, and emotively supercharged that many societies react to its sexual potentialities with sometimes drastic dread, manifesting in the form of rigidly adhered to incest taboos. For example, among certain aboriginal peoples, a father is not even allowed to look at his daughter from when she begins menstruation to when she is married. The punishment both father and daughter face for breaking this "taboo" is death. The same incest taboo is also true for mothers and sons and for sibling relationships, as well. The same extremity of punishment is, in fact, reserved for all forms of incest. In some cultures, for instance, young married males are not even allowed to have eye contact with their mothers-in-law. Yet there is one difference between the father/daughter relationship and all other incestuous couplings: the father's active participation in the sex act. In all other cases, the father, as guarantor of the law, imposes himself between the incestuous lovers. It is the father who comes between mother and son to separate them, and it is the father who comes between brother and sister. He performs a totally objective function. He carries out the law. He "separates" but is not, himself, involved in the act. In the father/daughter relationship, however, he is subjective, that is, he is, himself, one of the incestuous "lovers." Consequently, his function is to come between himself and his daughter. He must carry out the law and perform his "blocking" function even upon himself. He must separate himself from his own beloved daughter. This is no easy task. Indeed, the potential for incestuous disaster is so frighteningly imminent that we, who perceive ourselves to be so "civilized" and advanced, are only just *beginning* to deal with this sexually supercharged topic of father/daughter incest in our society. Yet it is this incest potentiality that, ironically, drives and structures the father/daughter relationship.

The father is, traditionally, his daughter's "first love." This "bigger than life" man is, in fact, her first contact with men. Life with her father, her "hero," is a magical time, when everything is new and exciting. She loves him unconditionally, and, in turn, he is free to love her in much the same way, *unrestricted* by the fear of usurpation his sons present. Remember, sons simultaneously represent the father's immortality as well as his mortality. The boy has the potential to carry on the father's genes, but the son's birth is, at the same time, the "first nail" in the father's coffin. Due to the inexorable processes of time, the son's ultimate victory over the father is ascertainable from the very beginning. Through his "identification," the boy will grow up to be like his father and "take his place everywhere." Nowhere is the paternal angst inherent in this process better presented than in Harry "Rabbit" Angstrom, the protagonist and comedic patriarch of John Updike's *Rabbit Is Rich*. Only after Harry discovers the "rubbers" missing from his nighttable drawer does he begin to resent his son Nelson's presence:

> *As long as Nelson was socked into baseball statistics or*
> *that guitar or even the rock records that threaded their*
> *sound through the fibers of the house, his occupation of*
> *the room down the hall was not more uncomfortable than*
> *the persistence of Rabbit's own childhood in an annex of*
> *his brain; but when the stuff with hormones and girls*
> *and cars and beers began, Harry wanted out of*
> *fatherhood.*
> (212)

In reaction to his son's growing sexuality, the father abandons his role as protector-provider to become, instead, a rival. The father senses his mortality in his son; when the boy is about, the scent of death is near. When Harry's wife, Janice, taunts him with, "I still don't know what you're trying to prove," in reference to her husband's sudden desire to whip himself into fighting shape, Harry's answer displays the intensity of his conviction. "'It's now or never,' he tells her, the blood of fantasy rushing through his brain. 'There's people out to get me. I can lie down now or fight.'" When she asks him who is out to get him, he replies smartly: "You should know. You hatched him" (142).

Conversely, the father's love for his daughter is not tempered by the love/hate ambiguity of the identification process inherent in the father/son relationship. Rather, the father can love his daughter wholeheartedly without fear of usurpation. The son has this same kind of unrestrictive love for the mother; however, when the boy's "mother love" becomes too dependent, it is the father's function to step between mother and son. He does so, for it is his paternal role to be the guarantor of family law. Therefore, when the daughter's love becomes dangerously excessive, it is his function to, once again, be that patriarchal guarantor. Consequently, it is the father who must voluntarily come between his daughter's love and, ironically, his own self.

Yet the potentiality is intoxicating. Let's return to Harry Angstrom, just for a moment. Feeling trapped by his Oedipal boy Nelson, "Rabbit" takes comfort in a fantasy that wistfully substitutes a daughter for a son. His affair with another woman, Ruth, long ago comes home to haunt him in the attractive figure of Annabelle, a beauty whom he believes to be his illegitimate daughter, although this is vehemently denied by the mother. Yet the possibility induces comparisons; with a son there is always the eager premonition of death reflected in the offspring's impatience: "Why doesn't Dad just die," questions Nelson, "People that age get diseases. Then he and Mom. He knows he can manage Mom" (323). But a daughter offers a more pleasing immortality, suggestive of incestuous sexual overtones. "Her eyes his blue: wonderful to think that he has been turned into cunt, a secret message carried by genes all that way through all these comings and goings all these years, the bloody tunnel of growing and living, of staying alive. He better stop thinking about it, it fills him too full of pointless excitement" (34). Well, pointless or not, he cannot stop his thinking about her or the excitement. "Harry thinks of the girl's long thigh as she stretched her way into the back seat and imagines he smells vanilla. Cunt would be a good flavor of ice cream, Sealtest ought to work on it" (21).

As the above illustrates, the severing of himself from his daughter is one facet of the paternal function that can be quite difficult to carry out, for – as the daughter's budding female body matures, she becomes attractive as a beautiful, *sexual* being – who loves him madly. To make matters worse, so early on in her young life, she often has only the father to "attract"; thus, all her "flirting" is directed at him. This flirting is very important to her sexual growth as it is an integral part of her building confidence in her femininity. Is she attractive? Can she get men to notice her? So she literally "practices" her flirting skills on the father. If he responds to her, that response reaffirms her "beauty" and desirability. It also provides her with the self-assuredness she will need when she encounters other men outside the family. Besides serving as a confidence builder and as feedback of her desirability, her flirting with her father also provides the daughter with an identity. In fact, it is her intense desire to please him that structures her *feminine* identity and shapes her *feminine* personality, especially as it manifests in her behavior towards other males. Surprisingly enough, it is the father who fashions his daughter's femininity and who determines how she behaves as a woman, for, don't forget, part of the paternal function is to provide his children, sons and daughters alike, with identities.

With sons, this is an easy process to understand. His sons find themselves through the process of "identification." When they identify with the father, they gain identities by assuming the paternal function. It is passed on to them. The father must be lost. And, in turn, the son must "also rise" only to be lost to his sons. Perhaps, Herbert Gold, in his sentimental remembrance, *Fathers*, intuits the proper metaphor, equating paternal ancestry to chinese boxes, "fitting into each other," for, indeed, like unique puzzle boxes, the father breaks giving way to the son; the son matures to become the father; and so on. But how does this work with daughters? How does the father shape his daughter's femininity?

This process is also easy to understand. The daughter wishes to please and to be attractive to her father, so she will do whatever it takes to make him happy. Consequently, if her father likes girls with pigtails who giggle and blush shyly, to attract him and secure his love, the daughter will wear her hair in pigtails and giggle and blush shyly. You see, it is the father who shapes her feminine behavior patterns because she fashions herself into what she believes is attractive to him. If the father likes girls who are "tomboys" and who climb trees, the girl will cut her hair short, hit baseballs, and climb trees. And so on. This desire to attract and please the father is only "natural," for this is how young girls develop the confidence and abilities to attract young men outside the family – by practicing on the father. The process is similar to baby birds flapping their wings in the safety of the treetops, building the strength and confidence to fly when the proper time comes to leave the nest. But, make no mistake, this daughter "flirtation" can be a dangerous game. This is why it is so important for males to mature *before* becoming fathers. The father must be mature enough to give up his own sexual desires for something bigger – his daughter's life and well being – than his immediate pleasure. When a male assumes the paternal function, it is his responsibility to come between himself and the love of his daughter with just the same intensity as he does when he comes between his wife and son.

Thus, fathers who abuse their daughters are not fathers. They may be biological "gene" donors, but they do not carry out the paternal function. So those who rail against patriarchy by illustrating the horrors of father abuse upon daughters are incorrect. Abusive fathers are never to be considered real fathers. They are, themselves, immature males abusing and bullying the daughters who love them. They are not men. And they are not fathers. Their sins are not sins of the fathers. Their sins are the sins of immature males, who have never reached paternity.

Male maturation is, therefore, the essential element. It takes a *mature* male to give up the nearly idealistic love of his daughter to another man – especially when he perceives these other men to be inferior to himself. This is why, when a woman gets married, it is her father who "gives her away." This ritualistic act that sets the marriage ceremony in motion is no symbol of male domination over women; it is not illustrative as some would have us believe of the daughter as chattel and property of the father being passed on to the husband's possession. Rather, it is an expression of the "giving" nature of mature masculinity. The father is demonstrating his unselfishness by letting go, "giving away," his claim to the love his daughter has bestowed upon him, so that she is free to give it again, totally and sexually, to her "new" love. This is why, traditionally, it is the bride's family who pays for the wedding. For, you see, viewed from this perspective, the role played by the "father of the bride" is revealed to be a "giving" one, a demonstration of the selflessness inherent in male maturity and not – as some may mistakenly believe – an expression of paternal control over, and ownership of, daughters.

XII

There is a great deal of confusion about the father/daughter relationship, so much so, that it has led to a tragic state of events in contemporary America – a cumulative catastrophe so devastating that I often wonder if we can ever recuperate. Before I explain, we need to explore the father/daughter relationship even further, for, I believe, it is at the root of the impending "armageddon" American society currently faces.

Before the paternal function was lost, in the traditional American family structure – shaped by the post-agrarian forces of the industrial revolution – fathers held positions both within and without the confines of the family household. Once the majority of society left the farms in favor of city life, fathers worked, traditionally, outside the home. Fathers went off, by themselves, to labor everyday and returned, it is hoped, in the evening. As a result, the father became a metaphorical "umbilical cord," so to speak, between his children and the rest of society. This paternal link to the external world was extremely important to his children, for through his example he provided his daughters and sons with the courage they needed to venture out and explore. In this way, the father functions as an "anchor" to his children, sons and daughters alike. They can hold safely onto him with one hand while exploring the outside world with the other. It is this entrance into society that is their first step toward achieving individual identities. The home is mother. And her realm is an important one for their early development; however, once they begin to seek independence, they must abandon the nest. As long as they are with her, they are unable to be weaned from her "oneness" and the loss of a separate "self" each child's lack of individualization entails. As long as they are her children, they are lost in a maternal whirlwind of collective "unconditional" love. In Barthelme's *The Dead Father* – a tour de force of modern day mythology – daughter Julie explains the paternal function in terms of its signification:

"The vagina, she said, is not where it's at" (76). Where "it's" at is the father.
"The fucked mother conceives, Julie said. The whelping is, after agonies I
shall not describe, whelped. Then the dialogue begins. The father speaks to
it. The 'it' in a paroxysm of not understanding. The 'it' whirling as in a
centrifuge. Looking for something to tie to. Like a boat in a storm. What is
there? The father" (77).

Julie's interpretation of the father's function is reinforced by the
forward of the novel where the Dead Father, literally, a "dead man," is
defined as "a log, concrete block, etc., buried in the ground as an anchor"
(4). The image of his children tethered to him in this manner cleverly
parallels their foetal relationship in the womb of their mother, where they
were tied to her by the umbilical cord as well as their relationship to her in
the home, where they are tied to her by her proverbial apron strings.
Succinctly, mother and father are positioned at opposite ends of the cord,
engaged in a tug-of-war battle over the children. If she wins, they remain
"as one" with her, indivisible from the maternal function, forever knotted to
the family unit, creating as son Thomas wittily snips in *The Dead Father*,
"zombies, psychotics, and warps...In excess of what is needed" (78). If the
father wins, however, the children are pulled free of the maternal whirlwind
and can, then, find their own identities separate from the mother. In this
way, he is the vehicle of their second birth – away from the family and into
society. What is most important to understand, however, is that the father's
victory comes about only because he, too, is willing to "sacrifice" himself
for the children. When the father successfully weans his sons and daughters
from the mother, he does so realizing their newfound freedom and
individuality are the "nails" in his proverbial coffin, as well. Like maternity,
his paternal function has also become superfluous. Rather, like maternity, it
is passed on to the children. His daughters, once they are free to procure
mature identities, will become mothers, and his sons – usurping his role –
will become fathers.

As important as this paternal function is to sons, it is even more
important for daughters because one day they may very well be overtaken
by the maternal function themselves and are, subsequently, forever in
danger of being sacrificed to it. Therefore, it is essential for daughters to
develop a personal, individualized identity, so they can assume the maternal
function and not lose their sense of "self." Consequently, there is a vast
difference between giving birth and being a mother. Nature provides every

woman with the ability to give birth; fathers help women achieve the maturity and identity they need to become mothers. Equally important is the father's support of his daughter. Her exit from the family can be a departure filled with fear and anxiety. She can even perceive it as one of abandonment and rejection. Remember, it is the father's function to come between himself and his daughter to sever the possibility of an excessive, incestuous relationship. Consequently, it is very easy for the daughter to misperceive the father's distancing of himself from her as rejection. It is also easy for her to believe his failure to continue to respond positively to her "flirting" is his sudden recognition and affirmation of what she has always secretly felt all along, that she is unattractive and has lost him to that "other woman," mom. This is why some women are attracted almost solely to the men of other women; it isn't the man they want – it is the "besting" of the other woman that they seek. So, when the father successfully performs his function, not only does he lose the one woman in all the world who loves him without reservation, but also he runs the risk of her being hurt or even angry. I wonder how many daughters are asking themselves why the great relationships they once had with their fathers deteriorated – especially as they reached young adulthood. And how many daughters "can't wait" to get out of the house! Is it any wonder that, today, young girls leave home earlier than their brothers do? And in greater numbers! The paternal function is grossly misunderstood.

Nevertheless, by continuing to serve as her "anchored" link to the outside world, the father demonstrates that males can, indeed, be supportive and that he does care for her; thus, his protective nature helps her develop a new trust in men that allows her to form a meaningful relationship when she leaves the family unit. Additionally, everyday life with father has allowed her to see what men are really like, so she doesn't have to create fantasy males – fantasy fathers and fantasy lovers. Fathers fashion a sense of reality about relationships with men for their daughters, so these young women can relate to men outside the family without falling prey to illusions and the tragedies of their resultant disappointments. Without fathers, in fact, daughters are often lost. They can become withdrawn and fearful. They can lack confidence. They can feel unattractive and unloved. They can form unhealthy dependencies and trust inappropriately. They can withdraw. Or, just as tragically, they can behave in a totally opposite, yet equally destructive, fashion. They can exhibit a "free floating" rebellion. Feeling "invisible," they can go "wild" and exhibit excessively self-destructive behavior in a tragic effort to be noticed – not caring what becomes of them or their children or the whole world, for that matter.

Obviously, daughters *do* need fathers.

XIII

So what is the problem? What has gone wrong? Unfortunately, there is a negative side of the father/daughter relationship, and it can be devastating to daughters. The father demands all his children follow *his* law. "As long as you live in my house, you'll do what I say." To reiterate, by setting down the "law," the father shapes the rules of the family and, by extension, society. This is how the child learns his or her place in the family and/or society and discovers his or her identity. In short, it is through obeyance of the father's law that we cut the symbolical "mother love" umbilical cord. Thus, it is the father's function to provide his children with an identity because getting an identity of one's own is an essential and elementary step in the process of separation from the mother. Simply put, the father comes like a "knight in shining armor" to sever the metaphorical "apron strings" that keep us connected to the mother, thereby freeing us to be autonomous individuals. So, I ask again, what's the problem? If the father is the "dominant" figure, if the father casts himself in the role of savior, if the father is the heroic "knight in shining armor," then who is the villain? Who is the symbolical "dragon"? That's right, mother!

This negative aspect of motherhood is repeatedly and powerfully illustrated in universal mythologies, perhaps nowhere more vividly than in India, where the ominous figure of "black Kali" – "earth mother" – represents the "devouring" nature of maternity. Black Kali is a powerfully horrific figure. She wears three necklaces, one of skulls, another of snakes, and one fashioned from the heads of her sons! She has earrings made of little children. She holds the severed head of a giant in one of her many hands, and her tongue is always dripping blood. Her rites involve sacrifice – early on, even human sacrifice – and she is associated with all kinds of devil worship. Yet what is most interesting about her identity is the fact that she is, herself, merely one form of the "Great Goddess," the eternal mother, to whom we must all return, be it via the tomb or the womb. She dramatically and colorfully represents the danger of losing one's individuality to the "consuming" nature of maternity. But she is not the maternal function; she is merely one facet of its vast and complex multiplicity.

Therefore, it is unfair and inaccurate to characterize motherhood in such narrowed imagery, implying that the sole purpose of motherhood is to be ultimately destructive. Nevertheless, when the father sets himself up in the dominant role as the rescuer of his children from what he perceives as the suffocating love of their "devouring" mother, the inference is that she and her "consuming" function are inferior to him and his liberating function and, by logical extension, that all women – because they will or may eventually assume the burden of the maternal function – are inferior to men. *This is the problem*! This is the destructive message inherent in the father/child relationship – especially in the father/daughter relationship. His sons grow up believing they are superior to women, that it's a "man's world" – a thesis quite bluntly illustrated by the Hebrew prayer, "Thank God, I'm not a woman" – while his daughters are conditioned to accept the "cold hard fact" that they are secondary human beings who are "nothing without a man." How is it phrased in *Genesis*? "For your husband shall be your longing,/though he have dominion over you" (3:16).

Be honest, what is the first question we ask a man when we are introduced to him in a social setting? Isn't it, "What do you do for a living?" Conversely, what do we ask a woman when we are introduced to her in the same situation: "Are you married? Are you seeing anyone?" There's a big difference in those questions. We are defining males by their ability to "provide" which, granted, is a bit of an unflattering and pressuring criterion; nevertheless, we are still judging a male by his deeds, by his accomplishments. On the other hand, we are defining females impersonally and unfairly, by their ability to attract males. So, when a daughter gets the message that she is a secondary player, the father's function becomes destructive. His identity is changed. Instead of perceiving him as her savior from the ravages of an evil "black Kali," she sees a "suffocating" father who is always the disciplinarian, always yelling, and never satisfied or made happy. She sees a man laying down hateful and hurtful laws. She finds herself confronting a man – all men – who must be opposed and defeated. She perceives a male society – a man's world – that is against her. And she's right. That destructive message has no place in paternity. A father who delivers that message is, in all truth, no father.

Consequently, if our society has been structured in the past by that "double standard," then we have never really experienced the paternal function in America. We have suffered, instead, under a perverted form of male domination which had to be expunged. Thus, the "patriarchy" women have rebelled against was a dysfunctional system and not indicative of the constructive nature of paternity. That system had to go, but it is unfair – and inaccurate – to call that system a patriarchy. Patriarchy is a positive, enabling structure. The diseased system we once had in America was not in any way illustrative of the greatness inherent in the paternal function. In light of this, we may honestly say America has yet to experience a legitimate "marriage" of maternal and paternal functions. For, from the beginning, what we mislabel as patriarchy in America was anything but.

For example, let's look for a moment at one of the most famous of novels, Nathaniel Hawthorne's *The Scarlet Letter* and its female protagonist, Hester Prynne. Hester is a woman trapped in a puritanical male society that has become too stifling, too much in opposition to nature, especially her feminine sexual nature. In fact, that is what this "mythology" is all about. And I believe I am correct in calling *The Scarlet Letter* a mythology, for its symbolism is understood by generation after generation even among those who have never read the book. Just say the words, "scarlet letter," and the heart understands the deeper, metaphorical meaning even without knowing the story. But what is the "deeper meaning"? *The Scarlet Letter* is all about the conflict between a woman's sexuality – nature – and an overly suppressive male society's inability to respond to that "call of the wild," her sexuality.

Abandoned by her "cold" and aged husband Chillingsworth, Hester falls in love with the puritan preacher Dimmesdale. Their "tryst" results in Hester's giving birth to their child, Pearl – whose very name hints at the conflict between the "natural" grain of sand at a pearl's core and the secreted glossy layer of mantling so valued by an artificially-structured society. As a result of her adultery, the town punishes Hester by making her wear a scarlet letter "A" on her breast. Hester endures this punishment, for she refuses to reveal the true identity of her infant daughter's father. Dimmesdale, a leader in this overly restrictive male dominated society, refuses to openly admit paternity of Pearl and, as a result, destroys himself inwardly, suffering from guilt and shame, in much the same way Hester suffers outwardly from public rejection and scorn. This is, for the most part, the major portion of the plot. It doesn't sound all that exciting by contemporary standards, does it? So why does this "mythology" have such power?

The scarlet letter "A" is a *sexual* symbol, the most powerful of sexual symbols, the female genitalia. There is no doubting the "feminine mystique" of the scarlet letter. It is woman, and we know it is woman. It can be worn by no other character in the novel. Furthermore, it is Hester's because of Hester's sexuality. Consequently, the scarlet letter A is a representation of Hester's sexuality – both figuratively and quite literally. Literally? Here's what I mean: When worn between the breasts of Hester, the scarlet "A" approximates the size, color, and shape of the female genitalia – as viewed from behind when the female "signals sexually" in true animalistic fashion, that is, when she lifts her rear end and directs it backwards to the male.

In nature, when a female wants to sexually attract a male, her genital region is visually presented backwards to him. Consequently, in the novel, the positioning of the scarlet letter "A" between the swollen, hemispherical breasts of Hester recreates the juxtaposition of anal and vaginal triangulation between the hemispherical swellings of the female rear end. Draw two circles side-by-side, then place the "A" between them, and you will understand.

Yet why is this so? Because humans walk upright, the female genitalia is invisible beneath the body cavity; therefore, nature – to compensate for the loss of that sexual signal – refashions the female human's breasts to recreate the hidden sexual signal. Is there really any doubt that the human female breasts are sexual signals? All other primates, because they do not walk upright, have flattened, elongated breasts with protruding nipples – the perfect design for breast feeding infants – all except humans, that is. The swollen, hemispherical breasts of human females oppose this function. Consequently, as Desmond Morris points out in his classic study on the subject, *The Naked Ape*, if design follows function, the human female's breasts are designed to follow the function of sexual signalling *not* maternal nurturing. "The enlarged female breasts are usually thought of primarily as maternal rather than sexual developments, but there seems to be little evidence for this. Other species of primates provide an abundant milk supply for their offsprings and yet they fail to develop clearly defined hemispherical breast swellings. The female of our species is unique amongst primates in this respect. The evolution of protruding breasts of a characteristic shape appears to be yet another example of sexual signalling" (70).

Too many dramatizations of the novel exaggerate – theatrically – the size of the scarlet letter. This is misleading, for Hawthorne takes great pain to describe the size and to elaborate on its enigmatic energy: "It was the capital letter A. By an accurate measurement, each limb proved to be precisely three inches and a quarter in length. It...was a riddle which (so evanescent are the fashions of the world in these particulars) I saw little hope of solving. And yet it strangely interested me. My eyes fastened themselves upon the old scarlet letter, and would not be turned aside. Certainly there was some deep meaning in it, most worthy of interpretation, and which, as it were, streamed forth from the mystic symbol, subtly communicating itself to my sensibilities, but evading the analysis of my mind" (27-28). He continues, "--I happened to place it on my breasts. It seemed to me--the reader may smile, but must not doubt my word,--it seemed to me, then, that I experienced a sensation not altogether physical, yet almost so, as of burning heat; and as if the letter were not of red cloth, but red hot iron. I shuddered, and involuntarily let it fall upon the floor" (28). As Hawthorne intuits, when placed in its "natural" position between the breasts of Hester, the "enigmatic" scarlet letter's shape and its "accurate measurement" approximate the size, color, shape and "heat" of the female genitalia as viewed from behind.

However, in the novel, Chillingsworth and Dimmesdale, true to their names, refuse the sexual signalling of Hester because of their desire, each in his own way, to sublimate their true "animal" male natures – their assumption of the paternal function – in favor of some loftier, more selfish identity: Chillingsworth in pursuit of knowledge; Dimmesdale in pursuit of spirituality. Hence, both – "chill" and "dim" – prove false to the sexual command of Hester and, by extension, to their masculinity and to their ability to assume the paternal function. Hester's name, itself, means "one who commands." To "hest" is to command; therefore, to be a "hester" is to be "one who commands." Chillingsworth is "cold" to the command while Dimmesdale refuses to "see" the "dale" or "valley" that is flashed before his eyes. Consequently, both men fail to assume the paternal function. Both men fall prey to its subversion by an overly puritanical male society that has nothing to do with a true patriarchy.

In this way, *The Scarlet Letter* becomes the screen upon which these inadequate males are displayed in all their immaturity for valuing the sublimations (knowledge and spirituality) of their overly puritanical society over the "natural" response they should exhibit as mature males to Hester's sexual signalling. Neither man can rise (pardon the pun) to the occasion, thereby revealing the crippling nature of an overly restrictive male society that emasculates its males, ironically, in its attempt to totally devalue its women, especially their feminine sexuality which it greatly fears to the point of equating that feminine sexuality with the devil. When this puritanical society degrades the natural sexuality of women in favor of misguided male notions of sublimation, it ironically destroys both the women it degrades and the men it tries to elevate. Chillingsworth and Dimmesdale are not "better" men because they seek the "higher" attributes of knowledge and spirituality over the responsibility of commitment to a sexual woman, Hester; rather, they are not men at all. And, more importantly, they cannot mature enough to accept the role of father. Despite the promise of power each man seeks through pursuit of his chosen sublimation, each man is shown in his immaturity. Each man demonstrates, in his own way, his "selfish" nature and his obvious inappropriateness to assume paternity of "Pearl." Neither man can sacrifice his quest for sublimation and the power it promises to respond to Hester's command to recognize and accept her sexuality as an *equal* force in the begetting and subsequent parenting of their child. The selfishness of both men makes them immature and, thereby, inappropriate to assume paternity – either biologically or societally – of Hester's daughter Pearl.

Therefore, Dimmesdale's exposure upon the public platform is, rightfully so, not the climax of the novel; rather, the action of the story ends where it begins with Hester and the scarlet letter and the "truth":

Women, more especially,--in the continually recurring
trials of wounded, wasted, wronged, misplaced, or
erring and sinful passion,--or with the dreary burden
of a heart unyielded, because unvalued and unsought,--
came to Hester's cottage demanding why they were so
wretched, and what the remedy! Hester comforted and

counselled them, as best she might. She assured them,
too, of her firm belief, that, at some brighter period,
when the world should have grown ripe for it, in
Heaven's own time, a new truth would be revealed, in
order to establish the whole relation between man and
woman on a surer ground of mutual happiness.
(185)

So it was "woman" – "unvalued and unsought" – who rebelled against the injustices of a puritanically corrupted poor excuse for a patriarchy! More specifically, it was the daughter, "wounded, wasted, wronged, misplaced," who sought to prove that women are *not* inferior.

But why now? Why, after all these generations – numerous generations before and after Hester's tale – of patriarchal control have daughters finally revolted to establish what Hester so accurately describes as "a new truth"? And why hasn't this "new truth" led to "establish the whole relation between man and woman on a surer ground of mutual happiness"?

XIV

Joseph Campbell once observed that there were two major influences on modern thought: Karl Marx and Sigmund Freud. Marx, according to Campbell, told us there were two kinds of people, the oppressed and the oppressors. And Freud, Campbell concluded, informed us that we were the oppressed and that our parents – especially, I would say, our fathers – were the oppressors. This got me thinking. The antiheroes of the 1950s, the James Dean "rebels without causes," the "wild ones" as portrayed in films by Brando on his motorcycle, were not the overthrowers of fathers. These "bad boys" were simply replacing the father's "law" with laws of their own. These sons desired to change paternal laws to please themselves. They sought, as all Oedipal sons have always sought, to take the place of the father and redefine the law in their own image. Their surface displays of "lawlessness" were fraudulent. Consequently, despite the flamboyance of their Hollywood style of deviant posturing, these boys were offering "more of the same," that is, either they represented the confusion and ambivalence of an Oedipal son, a "rebel without a cause," or, as "wild ones," they illustrated the chaotic frustration of gang mentality. Either way, all they sought to accomplish was a restructuring of the paternal function, not its elimination. These "bad boys" sought only – rightly or wrongly so – to minimize the pain of male maturation by glorifying, and refusing to give up, the rebellious nature of lawless adolescence. These "rebels" were simply trying to avoid the obligations and sacrifices inherent in patriarchy by staying forever "selfish" and "self-gratifying" boys. Therefore, it was in their interest to make sure, despite the "showiness" of their open rebellion against certain facets of paternity, that fatherhood itself maintained its dominance over maternity. The inexorable processes of time were on their side. Eventually, they would assume the patriarchal mantle. So they sought only to refashion the role, not cast off the cloak. No, it was not his sons who overthrew the father. As rotten as these "incredible Oedipal eggs" were, it was in their best interest to maintain the paternal function – for themselves.

I'm certain, therefore, that the loss of fathers and paternal law came about at the hands of angry daughters – angry, "oppressed," "frustrated," and "suffocated" daughters. Only his daughters could have overthrown the father. Indeed, these "daughters of the American revolution" have succeeded enormously, "beyond their fondest dreams." They have completely negated, and rightfully so, the mistaken notion that men are superior to women, and they have done so with a vengeance. And, perhaps, that's good. I say "perhaps" because, unfortunately, in their anger and zeal, they have gone way too far.

XV

Now, I am not saying I am against women, "feminists" or feminism for that matter. Quite the contrary. I am in favor of gender equality. The king is dead! Long live the King *and* the Queen! In fact, I firmly believe that the father's message, "women are inferior," was hurtful and oppressive and had to be expurgated. However, it is also my desire to be objective and feel it's time – if you will forgive the banality of this silly pun – to "call a maid a maid." One message of the American structure of paternity was wrong, not the whole system. Still, I do believe the women's movement to be just and necessary. Nevertheless, like many causes in life, although it may have been "paved with good intentions," it has unfortunately gone astray. It has derailed! Consequently – forgive the punning use of yet another cliche – "the daddy was thrown out with the bath water." In their justifiable efforts to right the patriarchal wrong, daughters, perhaps unintentionally, obliterated the father himself and, more importantly, the patriarchal function.

Tragically, in the process, both the negative and positive aspects of paternity were lost. Granted, we can all rejoice over feminine efforts to create equality between the sexes. Women and men *are* equal, and the excesses of the traditional, "diseased" patriarchal system were abusive to women and degrading – as *The Scarlet Letter* so aptly demonstrates. Any "right thinking" person, man or woman, should be glad to see that oppressive system corrected before the puritanical scarlet letter "A" became synonymous with the "A" in America. But, to me, *corrected* is the key word. It had to be corrected, not *eliminated.* Yet it has been expunged as thoroughly as some incoming pharaohs eradicated every vestige of the existence of their predecessors. Succinctly, the women's movement has gone too far, so much so, it has itself become, ironically, as oppressive and destructive as the perverted patriarchal system it opposed and defeated.

In fact it may be the cause of the so-called "hypocracy" of today's feminist movement and its lack of energy. When the patriachal system was discarded, "deconstrted", there was essentially nothing to take its place. Consequently, without any real identity, the feminist movement is suffering though a bit of chaos. In mythological terminology, they are currently in their "ashes" time. What does this mean? Think of Cinderella. Look at her name. What is the root? Cinder. What are cinders? Ashes! The contemporary feminist movement, like Cinderella, is in need of rekindling of its fires to effect a positive "makeover". You see, when feminists rejected all the rules, they left themselves without rules, and therefore, without direction -- in chaos, in ashes. The stregnth of the rebellion carried them for a while, but now the energy has disspiated, and they are without the previous impetus that fue;ed their righteous anti-male fires. Therefore, in order for them to rise out of the ashes, they need to be reborn with a new identity. Ironically, when they obliderated their fathers, they obliderated the means to achieve that identity. So now they are in desperate need of a fairy godmother. Where are the fairy godmothers? Within! nd that's where the feminist movement will have to look-- within -- for a new identity. There are no princes with glass slippers anymore -- let alone good "balls."

So, now, we are without fathers. And what does this mean? It means we, men and women alike, cannot find our identities. Maternity and paternity are complements, that is, pieces of a whole. Maternity wakes us up to the fact that we are all equal, but that is only half the story. Men and women are equal but *not* the same. Thanks to the rebirth of our feminine perspective, we have equality, but, on the other hand, because we have lost our patriarchal point of view, we have lost our individual male and female identities, so we do not recognize the differences inherent in our "equality." Men and women are *different*, and it is the paternal function to identify that difference. Maternity tells us we are equal; paternity says we are different. Together, they make us realize we are "equal" yet "different." Therefore, the difference is essential, as essential as the aspect of equality. Men and women fall in love because of the difference. The "world goes 'round" because of the difference. And as the French have so wisely put it, "*Vive la difference!*"

Without fathers, however, we cannot recognize the "difference." This is why, today, we are experiencing so many relationship difficulties and problems of identity. How can men and women form relationships when they are confused about their own gender identities? How many times have you heard or said, "I've got to find myself." You see, we actually sense the loss of "self" that is inherent in the loss of paternity. We intuit the need of all human beings to find and love ourselves *before* we can find someone else to love. We have it all backwards. We continually search for someone "special" with whom to fall in love, but that's wrong. What we need to realize is that our loving someone is what makes that person "special." You are special. Your love makes the person you love special. But you cannot realize this until you can realize your self-worth as an individual, until you can accurately define your personal identity. And part of our personal identity is our gender identity. When we lose the paternal function, we lose our sense of gender differentiation, of gender identity. Try saying, "Men and women are different." Do you feel guilty? Do you really believe it? If not, why don't you believe it? It's true, of course. And it's essential to each person's ability to find himself or herself that he or she accepts that men and women are equal but different.

Ironically enough, the loss of identity is more destructive to daughters than it is to sons, for males are, by nature, "selfish" while females are forever in danger of losing themselves in the "giving" nature of the maternal function. Succinctly, women suffer more from father absence than men do. In fact, the loss of the paternal function itself is far more damaging to females than to males, for without fathers young boys cannot mature, and, if young boys cannot mature, there are no men. Without men, women are forced to endure relationships with boys. This is another reason we are experiencing so many relationship difficulties: Women cannot find men who are mature enough to "commit." Commitment is a "four-letter" word to most young males. The "boys" are much more comfortable forming gangs instead of relationships because commitment to a woman requires a mature identity while joining a gang is an escape from the responsibilities of male individuality and adulthood. Furthermore, irresponsible males prey on women. Gangs prey on women. Women have become victims. Women are victims – so much so, that, tragically, many women today have actually and openly embraced the identity of "victim." In their desire for an identity, any identity, women have accepted victimization – simply to have a name, any name. Remember, part of the paternal function is to give his children names, so they can become visible and distinct from the "all else" – especially the "all else" that is mother. Consequently, daughters have assumed the negative role of victim to avoid the invisibility a female endures when swallowed up by the "at oneness" of maternal identification. Even though she, herself, may eventually assume the responsibilities of maternity, the individual female must still be weaned from the maternal function, so that when she is inevitably overtaken by the possibility of motherhood she is not drowned by it and lost to her "sacrificing" nature. She must achieve an individual identity separate from maternity, so she can later assume the maternal function without losing herself in it or to it.

Conversely, her brothers do not face such a dilemma. Their "natural" selfishness protects them from being absorbed by the paternal function. In fact, to them, patriarchy is always an elusive role. The crown of the father always seems to be a little too big, too loosely fitting. Sons never feel they can ever grow into it. Their fathers seem to have come from a greater realm, a land of giants. Look at classical mythology; remember, it is structured by and rooted in a war between the gods and the Titans, an earlier race of Greek giants who, though they are temporarily overthrown, are a constant threat. They are held down, for now, imprisoned in that shadowy underworldly realm of Tartarus; however, they are always a danger. Remember, too, the same situation occurs in Scandinavian mythology. The gods are always at war with the giants, whose victory over the gods at the end of the world and of time, *Ragnarok*, is – not so surprisingly – inevitable. These mythological interpretations of the father/son struggle for possession of paternity is brutally and painfully played out, too, in a modern day mythopoeic tale, Pat Conroy's *The Great Santini*. The novel's protagonist, Lieutenant Colonel "Bull" Meecham, overwhelms his cowed family by a relentless assertion of masculine, militaristic authority. In Bull Meecham, a magnetic figure who represents a Marine Corps stereotype but also transcends it, the father/son relationship seems a throwback to an earlier, archaic age, so much so that his son Ben can never hope to usurp his authority. Consequently, when Bull, a fighter pilot, is killed in a plane crash, Ben, dwarfed by his father's flight jacket, like a warrior's colors hanging loosely over his lesser frame, can never hope to free himself from his father's mythologized presence. The paternal function is something always beyond his reach. Yet, ironically, it is this lend-lease nature of paternity that protects Ben and all sons from losing their identities to it.

Sadly, this is not true for daughters, however. Without fathers, they are forever in danger of losing themselves to maternity. This is the theme of Kate Chopin's too long ignored masterpiece, *The Awakening*: Women must awaken to a sense of "self" separate from their maternal function. In the novel, protagonist Edna Pontellier – whose father refuses, because of his selfishness, to assume the paternal function – is forced to struggle against maternity in search of her identity as a woman. Edna is special, for, as Chopin says of her heroine, she is not a "mother-woman." Chopin explains, "The mother-women....It was easy to know them, fluttering about with extended, protecting wings when any harm, real or imaginary, threatened their precious brood. They were women who idolized their children, worshiped their husbands, and esteemed it a holy privilege to efface themselves as individuals and grow wings as ministering angels" (689). Rather than sacrifice the true function of her wings, Edna must come to realize her wings are made to fly. Edna is an artist, who intuits there is something "essential" in her, something that she cannot sacrifice, not even for her children: her sense of self. "I would give up the unessential; I would give my money, I would give my life for my children; but I wouldn't give myself. I can't make it more clear; it's only something which I am beginning to comprehend, which is revealing itself to me" (720). This is Edna's "awakening," and it is the awakening all daughters must experience. It is the individuality – the personal identity – children, especially daughters, come to realize through the "weaning" function of paternity.

Because patriarchy has been so denigrated in contemporary American society, however, daughters – even more so than sons – cannot achieve identities as individuals. They can compete against men, but that too is unsatisfactory because women want both the independence of a personal identity and the potential to assume the maternal function. They seek to be "better" women, not simply to "best" men. Look at the titles of women's magazines that have been popular over past generations. Would you be surprised to discover that *Family Circle* and *Better Homes and Gardens* have been among the top "best-sellers"? These two titles represent the feminine duality. At once, a woman needs to feel she is mother, at the center of the "family circle." But that is not enough. What's the key word in the other magazine title? That's right: "better"! A better home than whom?

Her mother? Other women? Fathers? Men? Better than them all! This need to be "better" is a woman's cry for visibility and a sense of self-worth. Contrast these two magazine titles to one of the best-selling male publications, *Playboy*. Are we surprised? What does that title say about men? Men are drawn to self-gratification and away from commitment while women, conversely, need both the selfishness of maintaining a "better" identity and the sacrifice of a giving maternal nature, encircled by her loving family.

Consequently, competing against men in a male world may provide women with an identity, but it is a male identity and one in conflict with maternity. Today's "super women" are only just finding out how impossible it is to be both a high-powered executive and a mother at the same time. Consequently, women are discovering they have lost both; they have neither a male identity nor motherhood. They are not better mothers than their mothers were. Their mothers were great mothers – Goddesses, in fact. Their mothers are now grandmothers – do you see the irony, "grand" mothers! Today's mothers cannot even hope to compare. They are guilty, in fact, because they denigrated their mothers and motherhood, itself. And they are guilty because they are not good mothers themselves. They are guilty over leaving children in day-care centers, about not making "home cooked" meals, about not being with their children enough. They are guilty when their children get sick because the children are exposed to large numbers of other children all day long instead of being at home with them, their mothers. Is this why they're willing to deny the power of their own motherhood, the importance of being the mother of their children, in favor of a "village" raising their children? What kind of woman so devalues motherhood that she actually believes others can do a better job of raising and, more importantly, loving *her* children? For isn't that what a village cannot do? A village cannot give each child the unconditional love of a mother. Raising children isn't the issue, loving them is. And who can love more than a mother?

You see, today's women are guilty because they're being lied to, and they know they're being lied to but, still, make themselves believe the lies. "Don't worry," they're told by social engineering experts, "quality time is more important than the quantity of time you spend with your children," but women know better. "It's not your fault," they're reassured, "it takes a village. You can't do it alone." Tell that to their mothers. Tell that to their children. Anyway, a village may help raise their children, but – you know what – who's there for *them*, for these women – for *their* needs? It's not the village women need; they need men who will love them, who wish to marry them and forge lifelong relationships with them, who wish to raise families. Despite what they're told, they need men – just as men need women. Ask any child if loving parents are preferable to being raised by a village. But, let me warn you, if you're afraid of the answer, don't ask. Just go on believing the lies. Or, better yet, blame others. After all, you are the *victim*. Isn't that what you've been told?

Succinctly, women today are frustrated and angry by their ever growing sense of invisibility. So, with nowhere else to turn, they embrace victimization. Now, it all makes sense. They cannot have "it all" because they are victims. It's no wonder they cannot succeed. Some horrible someone out there – more specifically, some insensitive "man" – is victimizing them. Thus, the problem isn't within; the problem is they haven't succeeded in completely eradicating men and the male world from the surface of the earth. There's still a "glass" ceiling! Thus, more deconstruction is the answer. For, as we all know, "Men are pigs!"

Yet, to me, there is an additional reason – a more revealing reason psychologically – why women have been so quick to embrace the notion that they are victims. Perhaps, unconsciously, when women portray themselves as victims, they are putting themselves in a position to be "saved." That is, ironically, they are creating a condition for the return of their original "hero," the father, to come, once again, like a "knight in shining armor," to their rescue.

XVI

Obviously, women suffer from father loss more than they may choose to realize. Without fathers to force young males to give up their selfishness in favor of committing to something bigger than themselves, mature woman are doomed in their effort to forge relationships with "needy," destructive boys. Indeed, immature selfish males are *everywhere*. And what kind of relationships are they capable of forming with women? Look at our high divorce rates, resulting in "single parent" households – mostly single mothers. How many lonely, struggling women are there? How often have you heard women complain, "There are no decent men out there. All the good ones are taken." How many women ask, "Why can't I meet someone?" How many conclude, "I'm never going to meet anyone. I'm just going to have to get used to living alone"? How many children today are themselves having children? How many are killing those children or abandoning those children? And what's the psychological motivation behind the concept of "deadbeat dads," if not immaturity and selfishness? How many middle-aged men are still unweaned from their mothers? How many still live at home? How many are unable to hold a job or, worse yet, how many have no desire to even seek employment? These middle-aged "boys" are undependable and dependent. Dependency is, in fact, one of the central problems in contemporary America – dependency on others, on drugs, on government.

But males don't *want* to be dependent. It is not in the male psyche. In fact, dependency is the fate – "worse than death" – of immature males who cannot find proper identification with the paternal function, for dependency occurs when the boy cannot be weaned from his mother and is, subsequently, forced to identify with her. And it is destructive to all individuals – males and females alike – as well as to society itself. Let's explore: To a young male, this dependency, this mother-identification, is, in a psychological sense, "castration," that is, in order to atone (be "at one") with the mother, the boy must abandon his possession of the phallus. Thus, identification with the mother is inherently repulsive to a son. The boy's preference for masculinity, that is, his desire to retain the phallus, is so dominant, in fact, that it views femininity as castration, perceiving the mother as a castrated male and, thus, as repulsive. Imagine the horror a little boy faces when he first views his mother naked. What's happened to her penis? This repulsion of the female is what drives the boy away from the mother in favor of identification with his father. When we think of the Oedipal complex, we believe incest is its defining factor; however, that's not exactly correct. Excessive mother-love, once stripped of its sexuality, lays bare the actual origin of psychoanalytical anthropology: the pre-Oedipal mother. Basically, it is *this* mother the child equates with castration.

In his monumental book, *Life Against Death*, Norman O. Brown explains, "What is given by nature, in the family, is the dependence of the child on the mother. Male domination must be grasped as a secondary formation, the product of the child's revolt against the primal mother, bequeathed to adulthood and culture by the castration complex" (126). Succinctly, what pre-Oedipal maternal dependence represents is a return to the oneness of self and other; thus, to embrace the pre-Oedipal mother is to give up the self. Essentially, to give up the self is to accept death. Therefore, castration, which equates the son to the mother, is effective because, to accept it, the self must accept death. Consequently, the boy abandons mother love not because he fears the father, because he fears identification with the pre-Oedipal mother, that is, "oneness," the "loss of self."

Ultimately, then, boys do *not* want to identify with their mothers. Boys are not happy their fathers are gone. Boys want and need their fathers. They need to identify with fathers to avoid the psychological castration dependency upon mothers forces them to endure. This is why I am certain his sons did not rebel against the father. The paternal function in America was not lost to the "wildness" of rebellious sons. No matter how much they may wish the father dead, paternal identification is essential to sons. Boys don't want to be dependent upon mothers or mother substitutes like drugs, alcohol, gambling – even sex. No normal, healthy young male wants to be addicted. A male wants to be independent and, ironically, that independent, mature male is the only one who is capable of forming a commitment with a woman. Mature male independence is, in fact, *the* necessary ingredient for a relationship. It is not the problem. It is the cure.

Dependent males are the ones who cannot form relationships because immature men mistake a woman's "giving" for indebtedness. So a woman in a relationship with a dependent, immature male feels she "gives and gives" and cannot understand why she isn't appreciated or why her man won't or cannot give in return. The answer is obvious. From the perspective of the immature male, the "giving" woman is saying, "I give to you; therefore, *you owe me!*" And owing is not something a selfish young male can tolerate, for dependency is selfishness and immaturity, but, most importantly, it is the loss of the male self. When these young males raised without fathers "take and take" without giving anything back, they are, ironically, asserting their desire to be "free" of their dependency upon women. Their refusal to "commit" or appreciate the giving nature of their female "significant others" is their struggle against being swallowed up by femininity.

If they had fathers, they could "break" from their oneness with, and dependency upon, their mothers. They could then find themselves as men and, in that way, be free to "commit" to a relationship with a mature woman without perceiving such relationships as their "death." Once a man has a mature sense of identity as a male, he realizes his "giving" to a woman is not the "giving up" of his masculinity. How many times have we heard women exclaim in frustration, "Men just don't get it!" Little do women know how *true* this statement is. Without fathers, men don't get "it," but "it" means the maturity inherent in the true definition of "masculinity."

Men cannot relate to women because they cannot identify themselves as men first. How can they "get it," when they aren't allowed to be themselves? Masculinity has been so denigrated in our society that all males have been reduced to boys, totally incapable of "getting it." To them, "getting it" means mindless sex with even more mindless women. They have no clue as to what a mature male is. Instead, in their futile efforts to understand what a man is without paternal role models, they can only rebel against what they can recognize as feminine, that is, "giving," to try to discover their manhood by the erroneous and inefficient process of elimination. The idea is this: If I reject everything that is feminine, what will be left is masculinity. In short, these immature males deny whatever is "female" in the hope that such anti-feminine behavior will, by default, make them male. So, if a woman "gives," then the immature male cannot give because that is what women do, and he will not be perceived as effeminate. He will take and take – all that the women can give, especially sexually. These confused, delusional boys believe sex – because from their perspective sex denigrates women – is the sign of a powerful male. Of course, they confuse power with maturity, so they have more and more sex at younger and younger ages, even in this dangerous time of AIDS and other sexually transmitted diseases to prove their dominance over women. What's more, they measure their masculinity by how *many* young girls they can impregnate. In our country today, boys play a socially destructive game to determine their male "pecking" order: He who makes the most girls pregnant in the shortest amount of time wins. And we lose. The girls lose. The children of these children lose. America loses.

Tragically, there's more. This male confusion leads to anger and violence – against women! Again, I turn to Norman O. Brown to explain, a man "takes" because taking is a denial of dependence. This "taking," says Brown, "transforms the guilt of indebtedness into aggression;" consequently, the immature male is "inherently aggressive" as an "obsessive denial of femininity" (280). Thus, the more a woman gives, the more a man takes and the more aggressively violent he becomes toward her, for the more he takes, the more he resents his indebtedness to her giving, an indebtedness which makes him – as he sees it – effeminate. To assuage his guilt and its subsequent dependency, he becomes ever more aggressive and violent. This excessive aggression leads to more and more violence against what he perceives to be the source of his emasculating guilt: the giving woman.

So why do women keep on "giving"? In light of all of the above, wouldn't it make sense for women to stop giving so much? But they cannot help themselves. Even when a man tells a woman that her excessive giving means nothing to him and is, in fact, destructive, she still keeps on giving – even intimately, sexually – because, without fathers, she has been overtaken by her feminine nature. She has no identity and no sense of herself as a valuable human being. How many times have we seen young girls interviewed on "touchy feely" daytime television shows and asked why they continue to "sleep with" a boy who treats them terribly and, worse, tells them – outright – that he doesn't even *like* them? On the air, the boy will humiliate the girl to her face and say he doesn't know why she still does it because he told her to "get lost" and, besides, he likes her girlfriend, at least for that week, anyway. As millions of us watch her humiliation, all she can do is shrug her shoulders and say something like, "I don't know. I just do it."

She has no sense of self worth! She is invisible! Her maternal function has overwhelmed her personal identity, and her "self" has been sacrificed to a lifelong round of endless, indiscriminate giving. Ironically, the more her giving nature leads to pain and suffering, the more she is convinced of her denigrated state and the more she believes her punishment is justified. Without the paternal function, she reduces herself to immateriality: No wonder so many young girls today have eating disorders; the thinner they get the more invisible they become, the less sexual, the less female, the less alive. Ironically, if one is not alive, one cannot be absorbed into the mother. Reducing the self reduces the importance of losing the self. Losing something anorexic – ever so slowly – is less traumatic than losing something spontaneously vital.

Furthermore, an eating disorder, like anorexia, has another very interesting side. In computers, there is an expression, "Garbage in, garbage out." Well, similarly, if one does not eat, one has nothing to lose, that is, the anorexic girl is not compelled to have to "give" up anything, not even the apparent worthlessness of digested food. Excreting and ingesting are equally effected by anorexia; therefore, the girl's refusal to eat is, simultaneously, a refusal to, ultimately, excrete. Thus, anorexia is as much about not "giving" anything as it is about not ingesting, or "taking in," anything. The anorexic is tired of giving and tired of having things put in.

Even more complex are the intriguing parallel connections among anorexia, eating and sexuality. Remember, through the womb, life is "transformed." The woman accepts her lover's seed and gives birth to his children. Nature is the controlling power. Nature overwhelms the female. Consequently, a woman cannot reject her womb, at least not physically, not anatomically. If she takes "something" in, she is eventually going to have to give something in turn. Her sexuality leads to maternity. But, on a metaphorical level, she *can* reject this "transforming" burden. Like sex, eating is also a "natural" transforming process; food is transformed into life-continuing energy. Anorexia, then, can be defined as the rejection of a natural transformation process. So, in this way, metaphorically, the anorexic young girl can reject nature and, simultaneously, her subsequent loss of identity, the loss of identity she is forced to endure without the paternal function. Succinctly, her refusal to eat is her attempt to gain control over nature and, thus, free herself from drowning in it. Ironically, her slow death through starvation is actually her painfully slow effort to establish an identity separate from nature, a symbolical identity, that would save her from being "swallowed up" by the transformational maternal function. She will reject nature even at the loss of her physical body; in fact, her desire is to shed nature's physical body to be free of its power over her and, thereby, be reduced to nothing but a "name," the symbolical identity she would have received from her father if only she could have identified with his paternal function. Anorexia, then, can be seen as father identification, that is, the girl denies her female "natural" body in favor of reducing it to symbolic stature, the name that is the gift of her father. When the body is gone, all that remains is her name. By physically negating one transforming principle of nature, eating, she believes she can negate, even if only metaphorically, the other transforming principle of nature, maternity, which she fears because of the loss of "self" it forces her to endure. Thus, her anorexia is a defiant controlling of nature and an affirmation of "self." In short, her refusal to eat is an expression of her desperate need to establish an identity separate from – in opposition to – the laws of nature, by doing what *she* wants, even if it leads, ultimately, to her destruction.

This, as extreme as it may be, is an example of what may happen when daughters cannot find identities through the paternal function. Remember, like her brothers, she too needs the paternal function to wean her from the loss of self inherent in the oneness of mother love, for it is the father who teaches her to be "selfish," that is, to be "self-concerned," and that it is "all right" to be "selfish" in this way, to give selectively or to not give at all – if that's what *she* wants.

To do what *she* wants, isn't that what fueled the sexual revolution and feminism in the first place? Yet why hasn't the daughter gotten what she wants? Why has her rebellion proved to be so unsatisfactory and, worse, so self-destructive? Why does her sexual freedom seem more destructive than liberating? Listen to the powerful words of Susan Minot, in her incredibly descriptive and brilliantly insightful short story, "Lust":

> *After sex, you curl up like a shrimp, something deep*
> *inside you ruined, slammed in a place that sickens at*

slamming, and you fill up with an overwhelming sadness,
an elusive gaping worry. You don't try to explain it,
filled with the knowledge that it's nothing after all,
everything filling up finally and absolutely with death.
After the briskness of loving, loving stops. And you
roll over with death stretched out alongside you like a
feather boa, or a snake, light as air, and you...you
don't even ask for anything or try to say something to
him because it's obviously your own damn fault. You
haven't been able to – what? To open your heart. You
open your legs but can't, or don't dare anymore, to open
your heart.
(1007-08).

She continues:

You do everything they want. Then comes after. After
when they don't look at you. They scratch their balls,
stare at the ceiling. Or if they do turn, their gaze is
altogether changed. They are surprised. They turn
casually to look at you, distracted, and get a
mild distracted surprise. You're gone. Their blank
look tells you that the girl they were fucking is not
there anymore. You seem to have disappeared.
(1008)

Without fathers, daughters are invisible and, though "fucked," unloved. For there is a big difference between the two. The sexual revolution and its "free love" had nothing to do with love because *free* love – like anything else given away for free – has no value, either to the person who "gives" it away or to the one who gets it. Love is special, so is the person who loves and who is loved in return. That's the positive side of the father's message, the positive message that has been lost. It is through loving her father and getting her father's love that the daughter learns she, herself, is worthy of being loved. He makes her visible. Furthermore, by living with her father, she learns what men are all about and how to relate to them. Through their intimacy, she learns to trust men – when they deserve to be trusted, that is.

Most importantly, from her father, she learns about the "difference" between men and women. Through her father, she receives an identity: a "name" and a role and place in the family and society. He is, in fact, her link to society. His love gives her the courage and self-esteem she needs to survive in the realm outside of, and away from, the home, so she doesn't fall prey to "lust" unless she wants to, unless it's her own.

Now, however, without fathers sons and daughters cannot be properly "weaned." Sons, fearing the loss of their masculine identities, strike out aggressively and violently against anything feminine in an effort to find themselves in the resulting void, while daughters are caught in a "giving" frenzy, so much so, they have lost all sense of identity and accept even the role of victim – just to have some visibility, any visibility. This is the "sick" society we currently endure in America, a dying society without the mythological function of fathers.

XVII

Obviously, all of us are losers. Masculinity is being thrashed and denigrated on every front. Males are being blamed for every atrocity from the beginning of time to now, deserved or otherwise. Every positive trace of manhood is being expunged from American culture. Even the "old world" roots of the patriarchal system are being redefined and purposely villainized in a mean-spirited and, oftentimes, inaccurate rewriting of our history. Try to remember the last time you heard our "founding fathers" praised for anything. Try to remember the last time you heard the term "founding fathers," especially from our news media or in our schools. Yet, ironically enough, none of this "male bashing" is really doing much to help women. Today's women are overworked, underpaid, and unappreciated. They are competing against men at the loss of their femininity; they are embracing the worst aspects of masculinity – like going to war – while denying the greatness of maternity. They pursue independence, only to find themselves more dependent on others than ever before. They are "married" to big government instead of husbands; however, their meager earnings are taxed by this uncaring, inhuman lover ever more heavily, while they receive only "drips and drabs" back.

Furthermore, they've denigrated motherhood, made fun of their mothers or other women who seek to be mothers, but, as working "single parents," they are more "tied" to their children than their mothers ever were. In the words of Shakespeare's Prince of Verona, "All are punished!" Yet what can we do? We cannot – we should not – return to the perverted patriarchal system we once endured. Under that system, women were truly suppressed and devalued. Women were perceived as inferior to men. The *difference* between men and women was recognized, but tragically the *equality* was not. No, we cannot ever go back. No, we do not want to return to that. Nevertheless, we do want to, somehow, restore fathers, for we – men and women alike – need their paternal function. So what can we do? Is there anything we can do, or is it hopeless? Is it too late to save America?

The answer may be a bit simplistic, but it is the only one I can offer. Part of our problem has been that we have confused the function with the person. In mythological terminology, we "concretized the metaphor." We mixed up our real fathers with the paternal function. Paternity is a metaphor, that is, the father is a "reference" to the many important aspects of his role – not the man himself. So, even if one's actual father is rejected, his function can still be recovered. Thus, we must restore the paternal function, regardless of what we may feel about individual fathers. For, no matter what, we must win back paternity. Fatherhood must, once again, be revered and respected. To do so, however, we must learn to distinguish between fathers and their paternal function. If you tell me, for example, that your father was cruel and beat you or abused you or shamed you without reason, then I say to you – yes – you are correct in your anger and your rejection of your father. Your father was cruel, and he beat you or abused you or shamed you without reason. But it is not *your* father we are talking about here. It is not *my* father either. It is no one's father. We are talking about the essence of paternity itself. Consequently, we must put aside our feelings about our biological fathers, good or bad, and embrace fatherhood – even if our fathers made terrible and hurtful mistakes. We can forgive them, maybe. But that's unimportant. They are unimportant. What is the issue here is the paternal function.

This is not to say, however, that the function of paternity is without fault. Remember, it has been, indeed, "flawed." At best, traditional "patriarchy" was, as we practiced it, an imperfect system as exemplified by Hester's puritanical society. In fact, this is why it fell, and why it deserved to fall. But we'll explore its faults momentarily. I want to take a minute or two, first, to clear up one point: When I suggest we should separate the paternal function from individual fathers, I don't mean we should close our eyes to the responsibility of each father to assume paternity and to successfully carry out the paternal function. Fathers who refuse to do so are derelict in their duties and deserve whatever punishment is reserved for such a heinous breech of responsibility. Mythology is, in fact, ripe with such examples of failed paternity and its resultant penalties. In classical mythology, Uranus, for example, grew so jealous of his children, he would not allow them to be born from their mother Gaia, earth. It became so unbearable for her that she persuaded their bravest son, Cronus, to castrate his father. Perhaps, not so ironically, Cronus, when he too became a father, refused to carry out his paternal function and had to be opposed, in turn, by his son Zeus. Fearing the loss of his supremacy, Cronus swallowed his children as soon as they were born. His wife, Rhea, tricked him by giving him a stone to swallow when their son Zeus was birthed. Then, when the spared and protected Zeus was strong enough to oppose his father, Rhea persuaded her husband Cronus to overcome his fear and vomit up her children. Believing he was safe, he acquiesced. When he did so, though, they rose against him and defeated him. This jealousy of the father towards his children is seen in countless mythologies all over the world. In Oceania, Tane, god of forests and birds – like Cronus – had to come between his father Rangi, the sky, and his mother Papa, the earth, to separate them, so he and his siblings could be born. And, in Egypt, Shu must perform the same kind of separation, only this time it is sky goddess Nut and earth god Geb.

We see this same pattern in current and recent literature, as well. The contemporary American novel is also filled with fathers who refuse to sacrifice themselves to the paternal function. We've already had brief glimpses of Conroy's "Bull" Meecham and Barthelme's "Dead Father," patriarchs who, refusing to give in to the inevitable victory of their sons, oppose their boys until the inexorable processes of time itself must intervene to defeat their selfish clinging to paternity. In the movie version of *The Great Santini*, if I remember correctly, there is an excellent example of father-selfishness. Every season, father and son play a game of backyard basketball – with the same result, the father wins. However, as time goes by, the son gets stronger and stronger while the father weakens. Additionally, the son has been practicing, so, when the day comes for the ritualistic backyard game of basketball, the father finds himself facing defeat at the hands of his son. To deny the boy his victory, "Bull" Meecham slams his son into the pole that holds up the basket and backboard – just as the boy was driving for the winning score. "Bull" may have maintained his string of victories over his son, but – in that act – he lost hold of the paternal function. Sadly, there are many others. The demonic Deacon Grimes of James Baldwin's purposely mythopoeic *Go Tell It on the Mountain* is an horrific example of a jealous father provoked to anger by his wife's acceptance of the "imperfections" he perceives in his "less than perfect" stepson, her homosexual son John. And Saul Bellow's *Seize the Day* is a dire warning of what may result from failed father/son relationships; in this insightful novel, the middle-aged adolescent, Tommy Wilhelm's maturation is "stunted" by the enduring strength of his rich and powerful father, Dr. Adler, so much so, that all overly dependent Tommy can do is "wait" in expectation of the day of his father's death, and suffer the taunts of his own guilty conscience for doing so.

The point is our fathers, in their mythological identities, represent the paternal "law," whether we like it or not and, more importantly, whether or not they deserve such patriarchal power. Ultimately, though, there is nothing to fear, for the paternal function cannot be possessed; it can only be "passed on."

XVIII

When daughters defeated paternity, America was quickly overwhelmed by the maternal function, and the denigrating patriarchal message, "Women are inferior to men," was just as rapidly replaced with the equally destructive, "All men are garbage." This is where we find ourselves today – women, like the men before them, "behaving badly," missing the point and believing, erroneously, they can find themselves by simply negating the "other." Men and women are complements; they each need the other gender. Thus, as we've come to realize, degrading one for the sake of the other is actually hurtful and insulting to both.

Nevertheless, for women, something had to be done and it had to be done quickly. The traditional patriarchal system was wrong, very wrong. Women had one choice, to be mothers. And, as we all know, one choice is no choice. Consequently, women were expected to assume the total burden of parenting. Women were expected to sacrifice their lives and their careers for children and husbands. Was that right? Was that fair? Let's be honest – no, it was not. All of the responsibility for raising the children should not have been thrust on the shoulders of women, simply because they are the birth givers. Giving birth to children and raising them are two different processes. Women are, by nature, the birth-givers, that's true. But giving birth, though completely in the realm of the female, is a relatively short-term process. Conversely, raising children, being a parent, is a lifelong process. Therefore, the decision a couple should make is not about having "babies" – a short-term process falling almost exclusively on the female; the decision a couple should make is whether or not they want to become parents – a shared, lifelong experience. Furthermore, the traditional patriarchal system was a response to a society that has long since passed us by. Because we were once an industrial nation, many jobs required great physical strength, so men worked and women stayed at home. Now, we are a "service" nation where men and women, alike, can perform most work functions. The traditional work paradigm has shifted, so too has the societal model.

Most importantly, however, in the traditional patriarchal system, when the father set himself up as dictator or, worse, as the "savior" of his children, he cast the mother in the villain's role, thereby making her inferior to him and, by extension, all women inferior to men. And, when women are made to believe they are nothing without men, both genders suffer. Therefore, I repeat, the traditional patriarchal system was wrong, was outdated, and was, consequently, doomed to inevitable collapse. However, the "male-bashing" system that has eclipsed it is just as wrong and just as doomed to inevitable failure. The signs of its demise are, in fact, everywhere visible in the dissolution of our society and the ever diminishing quality of American life. But, to me, nowhere are the inadequacies of an unrestricted maternal philosophy more evident than in government and the political arena.

The battle in America over liberalism and conservatism is really one of masculine versus feminine perspectives. When we praise the merits of big government, for example, we are actually displaying a maternal viewpoint. Conversely, when we suggest government should play a restricted role, we are really exhibiting a patriarchal bias. You see, the issue comes down to this question: Is it government's role to love and protect all of its "children," that is, its citizens, unconditionally, from "womb to tomb" – whether or not they have worked for or even deserve such support? Maternity says yes, of course. What else can we do? Paternity says no, let them earn it! Maternity, therefore, insists on an equality of result while paternity defines equality in terms of opportunity. Maternity says government is responsible for its citizenry. Paternity says government's only responsibility is to allow its citizens the ability to be responsible for themselves. Think about it: Aren't these the differing perspectives America is now in the process of debating regarding the nature of Affirmative Action, as well? Is Affirmative Action designed to provide equal opportunity (the paternal function) or equal results (the maternal function)?

The maternal and paternal functions are also at the root of the two major social philosophies currently "battling it out" in contemporary America. When America was dominated by a strong patriarchal system, it suffered from a paucity of maternal input. This "lack" needed to be filled. After all, "Nature abhors a vacuum." So "socialism" and its "unconditional" perspective took root to challenge democracy in America. And it grew quite strong, despite its failure around the rest of the world, because it was a vague representation of this country's missing femininism. But, now, ironically, the lack of a "conditional" paternal perspective caused by the socialistic nature of excessive feminism is creating a rebellion, a "backlash," against "quota" systems, "political correctness," social programs, big government – the trappings of socialistic thought – in favor of a growing "libertarianism" and a *laissez faire* attitude. Tragically, though, the struggle between maternal and paternal perspectives, though containing the potential for energetic movement and subsequent constructive change, can also be destructive to a nation; for example, the "standoff" has resulted in the emergence of an enormous amount of "apathy" in contemporary America, especially evidenced by the low turnout of voters when political elections are held. And the polarization of the differing maternal and paternal functions has resulted in a fractionalizing of the nation or, more accurately, an extreme polarization. On one side, we face the "deconstruction" of Americans into hyphenated groups: African-Americans, Italian-Americans, et al. – while, on the other extreme, we are forced to endure the formation of vigilante groups and militia organizations.

Other examples of government as the battlefield between maternal and paternal functions are the policy issues of time and resource allocation. For example, what is the proper focus of government: domestic or international politics? Fatherhood is extremely concerned with the "bigger picture," that is, the world view; thus, conservatism is highly patriarchal in this respect. The paternal function is a link between home and society, between family and "making a living," so economics, especially international economics, is a major concern. The "provider" does not want any interference from government, not ours, not anyone's. The patriarchal conservative wants the largest marketplace he or she can get while, simultaneously, resisting taxes, "caps," quotas and regulations – any kind of government interference. Additionally, because paternity is equally concerned with "protection," it furthers an "us" and "them" mentality, stressing the vital importance of assessable and "verifiable" peace treaties with foreign powers and, most importantly, it insists on the need for a strong and effective military. There is a basic mistrust of foreign motives with trust coming about slowly and only after it is earned.

The maternal function, conversely, is nurturing; what we call liberalism is actually maternity's focusing, especially in light of such extreme father absence, on the need for government "social" programs to fulfill the protective and provisioning responsibilities our emasculated males are currently failing to supply. In a sense, "big" government becomes a substitute for the paternal function and for husbands. The focus is heavily domestic, stressing satisfaction of the missing masculine supporting functions, provision and protection; consequently, the liberal emphasis is on socialized medicine, time off from work, child care, "safe" streets, flex hours, welfare, care of the elderly. There is a great deal of clamor for "support groups" to ensure the "safety in numbers," the herding instinct, that maternity requires in the absence of mature protective and provisioning males. Even the military is transformed into a support group, where the focus is shifted away from waging war to acceptance of fringe social elements and accommodation of less than battle ready recruits. There is a feminine sense of consciousness that the military is really a barbaric concept which would simply dissipate if it weren't for the "macho" aggressive nature of males. The belief is, if we trusted others and learned to "talk" and communicate, there would be no need for a military.

Even the battle over education is one of paternal versus maternal perspectives. Without fathers, of course, liberalism is everywhere dominant in our public schools and getting stronger everyday while, ironically, the academic quality of our school systems is geometrically weakening. Nevertheless, even though they are "shouting into the wind," conservative patriarchs do continue their futile call for "back to basics" and the need for competition while unchecked "unconditionalists" busily expunge all ideas of judgment, testing, and standards from our schools. From my ironical tone of voice, can you guess who's winning? Grades are abandoned for fear they may traumatize students. Self-esteem is the lesson of the day, that is, when there isn't a demonstration of condom usage. Curricula are refashioned away from academics to center around what children *want* to learn rather than what we *tell* them is correct. For, understandably, who are we? Who do we think we are? How dare anyone, in this "progressive" nation, declare his or her preferences or belief systems to be better than anyone else's! Everything is relative. Everything is equal and acceptable. Still, it must be recognized here, at least – if nowhere else – that, despite the countless introduction of one liberal program after the other, our schools are in critically desperate shape. Why? Because all these great ideas come from a "gang" of progressive educators whose entire existence depends on the constant introduction of ever more "new and improved" ideas – making them rich and our schools poor. Change has become, in and of itself, the important issue. As we build our "bridges" to the 21st century, we must be constantly and forever changing as if "progress" is simply a process of continual change. And have we ever changed! Our public school system was once one of the greatest systems in the world. Now, it's a disgrace. Schools are no longer interested in education. They are now social institutions bent on effecting ever more and more "change."

Fortunately, our colleges and universities have resisted this insanity a bit, so they are still (though barely) institutions of higher education. However, even they are under attack by the very same liberal ideas that, ironically, ruined our public schools. And, are you ready for this, the latest "progressive" idea, and – no, it didn't come from Chairman Mao, though it could have: The problem with America's colleges is the professors, the "intelligentsia." Too many of them are – can you believe this? – academics. Too many of them are researchers. Too many of them are scholars. So the idea is to replace these "elitist dinosaurs" with "high tech" computers, learning facilitators, the Internet (education's panacea), and – of course – ever more and more administrators and ever more and more progressive change! Let me be the first to say "goodbye" to our once superior American system of "higher" education. It seems that, in the middle of this, the famous "information age," the only thing we're losing is wisdom.

XIX

Traditionally, since the pioneering efforts of our "founding fathers," America has been more conservative, that is, patriarchal, in its thinking than liberally-minded or maternalistic. However, there were always signs of the inadequacies, even cruelties, inherent in an overbearingly one-perspective system. We can go back even before slavery in the South or even before the American Revolution to the Salem witch trials or to Hester Prynne's puritan nightmare. We can point to the atrocities that led to the Civil War, to the need for a women's suffrage movement, to the need to enact child labor laws, to the rise of labor unions, to the Great Depression, to the New Deal and the struggle for Civil Rights. Remember, either system, patriarchy or matriarchy, is doomed to failure by its own monomaniacal perspective, so it doesn't matter when or where the fall of our dictatorial patriarchal system began; in truth, the seeds of its destruction were always there, sown even in the fields of its earliest victories. It doesn't matter if the "fifties" or the "sixties" or the "seventies" were the turning point – be they the 1770s or the 1970s. The "point" was always turning. Vietnam – even Watergate – were just a couple more twists of all the multitude of turning points. The only thing that matters is that America's diseased patriarchal system did, inevitably, fall – as well it should have. But, now, we are without fathers – and suffering greatly for it.

Consequently, the equally monomaniacal nature of today's overly excessive maternal perspective in America is rapidly falling prey to the same type of intolerant, prejudiced forces that brought down the paternal function. For example, let's start by looking at the once proud concept of "free speech." I don't care what anyone says, free speech no longer exists in contemporary America. "Political Correctness," the maternal wish that no one should ever offend anyone else, has not only stifled the *vox populi*, but also the voices of individuals. Americans are now punished for something they have, or may have, said. Listen, I'm not defending what those who have been punished may have said, for that's "neither here nor there"; rather, I am defending their right to free speech without punishment, their right to say it – even if it is offensive, or if I may happen to disagree with it. Who would have believed that Americans could be fired from their jobs, hounded out of office, or publicly punished and chastised for what they said? And where is our sense of humor? I actually heard one female television newscaster sternly and brutally criticize comedians for daring to joke about liberal politicians. Isn't it ironical that comedians, who have always feared being silenced by the conservative right, are now facing real censorship from the humorless and intolerant "politically correct"? I'm truly frightened, first talk radio, now comedians.   How long will it be before our American children are instructed to turn in their parents for things said in the privacy of their own homes? I fear, it will probably be happening by the time this goes into print.

Yet there are more "chinks in the armor" of maternal liberalism and progressiveness, for example, the notorious "spending frenzies," the infamous, well-intentioned "generosity" of "tax and spend" liberals who, with all good intentions, wish to redistribute America's wealth. To conservatives, wealth is the glory of the capitalistic system and a mark by which the individual's success can be measured; however, for liberals, wealth is something to be dispensed with, apportioned to whomever is deemed most needy, as a symbol of atonement for the past evils of a capitalistic system that may have been blind to the possibility of former immoral and unfair means of accruing that wealth. Thus, the philanthropism inherent in liberalism is an expression of the progressive's self-righteous moral disdain for his or her country's patriarchal heritage of privilege based on unrestricted amassing of fortune. The maternal belief in unselfish giving, the liberal disbursement of taxpayer monies, then, is really a psychological mechanism through which they can retaliate against that "loathsome" patriarchal form of government they detest. In fact, much of the debate over spending and entitlements in American government today is really a struggle between the paternal and maternal functions as to whose value system is most truthful. In Washington and in the media, purposely mislabelled conservative rapacity is contrasted against unrestricted liberal philanthropism to determine which best describes the American identity. Ironically, this struggle over money – when translated into an Oedipal vocabulary – reveals the true quest for monetary fairness to be an insatiable desire for *power* and anything but an "unconditional" desire to give.

"Taking" control over large sums of money is actually an expression of the need for power. Let me return again to Norman O. Brown, whose explanation here ends in a quotation by Rushkin, "Classical economic theory, with its model of perfect competition, ignores the factor of power....'What is really desired, under the name of riches, is, essentially, power over men'" (249). Money is, indeed, power. And the power of wealth is its endurance. Money is perceived to be eternal – immortal. As Shakespeare intuited, money is the "visible god" of this world. Therefore, the liberal wish to "give" money is a thinly-veiled disguise for liberalism's true desire to have control over money and, thereby, gain its inherent "power," without having to suffer the guilt a more open and direct quest for that power would cause. Consequently, what is really "shared" through the showy largess of liberal "giving" is guilt. Declaring the psychology of economics to be the psychology of guilt, Brown asserts, "In the archaic institution of the gift, what the giver wants to lose is guilt" (266). Thus, liberal philanthropism can be understood as a desire to dissipate guilt by sharing wealth. "Money is condensed wealth; condensed wealth is condensed guilt" (Brown 266). Beneath all its flamboyant display of generosity, liberalism's apparent demonstration of maternal identification, that is, its "giving" away, and redistribution, of wealth, is an effort to resolve the guilt that comes from suppressing its real motive, *the selfish acquisition of power.* "In psychoanalytical terms, the gift complex resolves guilt by identification with the mother....In the gift complex dependence on the mother is acknowledged, and then overcome by mothering others" (Brown 280).

Ultimately, then, liberalism, especially its most progressive wing, denigrates its identification with the maternal function when it pursues its wish to have power over others – disguised always by the "best of intentions" – without having to suffer the guilt inherent in such a self-serving desire. When liberalism gives, it sends an unwritten message of indebtedness to those beneficiaries of its largess: "I give to you; therefore, you owe me." Thus, giving provides the giver with an enormous amount of power over the taker and creates, at the same time, a dependency that keeps the taker in an ever subservient role to the giver.

XX

Yet, despite its obvious hypocrisy and repeated bureaucratic failures, liberalism survives – even in its most oppressive, virulent form, socialism – virtually unchallenged by the American mainstream media. It is, in fact, protected and embraced by that media. Why? What was once a proud impartial system of news reporting – the best in the world and the freest, in fact – has now deteriorated into a "left wing" propaganda machine, whose cautiously crafted and meticulously measured messages have usurped the mythopoeic creativity and democratic vision of America's once "free" press. Again, why? Because of progressive liberalism's perversion of its identification with the maternal function! You see, for those who were most hurt by the "sins of the fathers" inherent in the paternal function – and there were many – liberalism is perceived to be the only viable alternative to patriarchy. Make "no bones about it," the paternal function, in its most destructive form, is restrictive and hurtful. In its perverted form, it suffered no tolerance for women, many minority groups, and homosexuals. So, under those conditions, even if one of the "excluded" may agree with the ideas and ideals of conservatism, that philosophy's identification with the negative facets of the paternal function made it unpalatable as a political choice. This is, indeed, an American tragedy! A "pox on *both* our houses"!

Nevertheless, what is particularly stressing to the fabric of contemporary American society is the "unholy" alliance forged by feminism today with even the most excessively marginalized systems of liberalism, for example, socialism. Because the maternal function requires an unconditional acceptance of everyone and everything, regardless of any precluding factor, women have found themselves in uncomfortable alliances with some quite unsavory elements. Nowhere is this "filthy bargain" more evident than in the way organizations purporting to represent women abandon females at the proverbial "drop of a hat," in favor of the most extreme "left-wing" causes. The issue of sexual harassment, for instance, becomes one of who is harassing whom, rather than focusing on the tragic harmfulness of harassment itself. If the harassment finds its origin in a liberal suspect and the subject of that harassment happens to be conservative or have conservative support, these women's groups will either stay silent or come to the defense of liberalism, even the most progressive forms of liberalism, not women. If the reverse happens to be true, however, and the defendant is conservative, then the very same groups will suddenly discover a reborn "feminism," the insincerity of which is painfully obvious.

To its detriment, another incident of hypocrisy illustrative of the unfortunate alignment of feminism with anti-American interest groups is the feminine support for, or failure to oppose, extremist minority groups, domestic or foreign, who are – themselves – radically patriarchal and fanatically suppressive of women, more so than any patriarchal system that ever previously existed, real or imagined, in this country. Furthermore, women's groups will openly tolerate and even make excuses for brutish male behavior from minority males while, simultaneously, attempting to castrate any chauvinism – perceived or otherwise – exhibited by "targeted" mainstream American men. Tell me, how can radical feminism rationalize an embrace, or at least a tolerance, of one minority religious group's "million man march," while, simultaneously, opposing a strikingly similar male "gathering" and "promise keeping" from the "religious right"? Actually, feminists should want to embrace both of these organized male movements. After all, why be afraid of "strong" men with strong religious convictions? These men are not the predators who ravage women. Males are derided for "fearing strong women." Shouldn't radical feminism be equally derided for fearing "strong men"? Obviously, gender has nothing to do with many of these feminist organizations. Why else do they wholeheartedly support Anita Hill yet abandon Paula Jones? Why else do they condemn Clarence Thomas yet embrace Bill Clinton?

Example after example of feminism's unhealthy alliance with left-wing radicalism present themselves once the destructive hypocrisy is brought to light: Because of the maternal need to unconditionally accept all perspectives as equal, no matter how damaging, liberal America is now falling prey to a justice system that is as much concerned with the race and rights of criminals – even rapists and murderers – as it is with their victims;

school systems that replace instruction in the "basics" with demonstrations of condom usage, a rewritten history, and lessons in tolerance – as long as that tolerance does not get extended to mainstream male perspectives, conservatism, any religiosity, or Western culture, especially that body of knowledge comprised of the products of "dead white males," of course; and, ironically, a dissolution of the family structure brought about by a redefinition of "family" and "marriage," *sans* men.

"Without men" seems, in fact, to be the battle cry of a militant feminism that is really more about lesbianism and socialism than women's rights – which is *fine* if everyone involved is honest about it all. Don't claim an organization's purpose is one thing while it's actually another. The two overlap, definitely; however, they also diverge. My point is let's be honest about the areas of divergence. Now, before I am misunderstood: I do not believe it is fair of anyone to equate homosexual rights in this country with socialism and the anti-democratic "deconstructionists," who wish to destroy America. An adult's sexual preference has absolutely nothing to do with his or her patriotism or politics, for that matter. Gays have sacrificed and fought for this country and earned, sometimes at the price of their lives, the highest of awards or, more tragically, have gone unrewarded and unrecognized for their valor. The same is true of minorities! I am a firm believer in an America that makes room for *all* its citizens. I believe in a democratic system that respects differences, not shuffles them under the rug. My America is a "choir," composed of many different voices – a harmony.

Consequently, even though the issue here is "feminism" and its "derailment," everything I've said positively about the women's movement can also be equally applied to minorities and homosexuals. The traditional patriarchal system was hurtful to them as well as to women, and they all had every right to oppose and defeat it. What I am railing against is the subsequent alliance of those who, at first, legitimately challenged the inequities of our American patriarchal system but who have now come to embrace – knowingly or unknowingly – the enemies of this nation, enemies who have nothing whatsoever to do with correcting the injustices – the failure to observe women's rights, minority rights, gay and lesbian rights – of our former diseased and unfairly restrictive system but who have, rather, everything to do with just one thing: the defeat of democracy in America.

Again, I do not want to be misunderstood. I do not wish to silence any voice, not even socialism. America cannot be America if it does not allow every point of view its freedom of expression. However, freedom of speech in America does not include the guarantee of an audience, or should it. Therefore, it is the right of every American to not purchase the newspapers that "blame America first" and to not watch the evening newscasts that promote the extreme liberalism undermining the fabric of our society. Don't go to the movies that rewrite history, that propagandize. Oppose the "progressive" school systems that are socializing our youth instead of educating them. Respect your individuality and trust in yourself before you allow yourself to become dependent on the charity of others, especially gangs, especially that "brother gang" in Washington called "big government." Be independent! Think and speak for yourself!

For too long now, we have allowed these propagandists to tell us what to say and how to think. As a result, we have allowed ourselves to be silenced by their words. We have marched to their drum beat, danced to their music, accepted in "lock step" the inanity of their slogans. They have replaced our dreams with their "catch" phrases. They have usurped our mythologies with their political correctness for too long.

Don't you see, there is nothing wrong with fighting back. Even the pacifist Christ, who preached the doctrine of "turning the other cheek," acted swiftly and violently when he saw the house of the Father defiled by the tables of the moneychangers. Our American house is being defiled. Do not be afraid to defend it. Too many Americans today no longer identify with this nation; rather they daydream of "fleeing" to a new land, a new America somewhere. Well, wake up! "You can run, but you can't hide." This is America. And it's damn well worth fighting for!

How can I make it any clearer? Males in America, including white males, are *not* the enemy! So there is no reason this country cannot become whole again. We can atone. We still have the chance to do it right this time, to get democracy right. Men, women, minorities, gays and lesbians – we *are* America. Unite as Americans, not as hyphenated Americans. Rewrite the American dream, so it includes all those who have a dream. What's wrong with a nation where "all men and women are created equal"? Just because you are disappointed or angry, do not allow yourself to be aligned with those who hate this country, who will be happy only when they see our once great nation brought to its knees – to be replaced with what? Have you ever travelled to socialist nations? Do you ever want to live in a communist country? Did you note the cheering crowds in Cuba, screaming to celebrate the visit of the Pope and the hope of a reinstitution of religion and spirituality in their lives his mere presence promised? Think, on how many fronts is religion being attacked in America? And when are you going to defend your religion? Remember, a nation without religion is a nation without hope.

I know you're angry, but your anger stems from injustice. Correct that injustice. Do not allow your misplaced anger to destroy America. In America, it is "all right" to burn the American flag. Where else is there such an extreme freedom? But, remember, it's all right to salute that flag as well, to pledge your allegiance to it. And it's all right to display that flag proudly. I suggest you do so, before you lose that right and that flag and for all it *can* stand, "one nation under God *and* Goddess!"

Besides, "who is kidding whom?" Socialism is a failure – everywhere, all over the world. The only place it thrives is among our liberal intelligentsia, who do not live under the very progressive system they seek to promote, who – ironically – could never themselves survive as socialists, for most of them are among the wealthiest people in America and live privileged existences, far removed from the common "rabble." The most liberal Hollywood jet-setters build walls around their estates. The most liberal politicians live in secluded and secured "compounds." The wealthiest liberals buy up secluded islands and real estate in foreign lands to which they can flee when this country collapses. Think about it. Socialism is a system that can only be *forced* on a people because the equality for "everyone" socialism promises always comes at the cost of individual freedom. All are reduced to the lowest common denominator. The great "many" have an "equal share" of "next to nothing" while the leaders control everything – and these dictators cannot be removed by democratic elections or peaceful means. Wake up! Just look at the rest of the world! What do you see? The birth of democracies – people giving their lives for the freedom we now take for granted, for what we are allowing to slip through our fingers. Now, look at the countries where the most civil rights violations are occurring, where people are treated the most horribly. Where are all the atrocities occurring? It's not America, as our enemies would wish you to believe. Be honest. Are these inhumane countries even remotely "democratic" nations? You know they are not!

We *can* live the American Dream, for it is the most "natural" of all human political systems, for what is democracy if not the "marriage" of men and women as equals. Different voices, differing opinions, but each enjoying equality. Democracy is not about agreement. It is about tolerating, accepting and respecting disagreement. Democracy does not sing with one voice – that's socialism on the left and fascism on the right. For, remember, "one choice is no choice." Democracy is a harmony of many voices, each allowed to contribute its wealth to the world. The paternal and maternal functions that shape our society are themselves "naturally" democratic in structure. They always have been. We shouldn't be seeking "bipartisanism." Rather, we should be encouraging the equal but different voices to forever ring true and loudly. We need only to revitalize the potentialities of our mythic vision to understand. The great mythological epiphany is an "awakening" to the truth that opposites are revealed, ultimately and ironically, to be the *same*. All the separate colors of the rainbow are contained in a single beam of light which is itself, though it illuminates all else, invisible – yet light is, ironically, all we can see. Everything else is invisible and only perceptible for its ability to reflect light. All physical vision, in fact, is dependent on the coming together, the interplay, of invisible and visible complementary opposites: shadow and light. Similarly, fathers and mothers are complements of a single entity, humanity itself. Human life cannot exist without both. Each cannot exist without the other. Glorify the "opposing" voices. Let each "ring out." For each makes the other whole.

Mythologically, the paternal and maternal functions are complements of a "whole" which is, ironically, always "more than the sum of its parts." Rising out of its mythopoeic vision, America is, likewise, such a "magical" coming together of complemental opposites. Look at the back of any dollar bill. The sloping sides of the pyramid – across from the Great Seal of the United States – are illustrative of this mythological insight; they meet, come together, at the eye of inner vision, the mythopoeic eye. And, when we pray, aren't we doing the same thing? When we prepare to address the "mystery of mysteries," we put our hands together, combining opposites – left and right – into "one." In this same way, the glorious spirit of America is born out of the coming together of its complementary opposites, an *e pluribus unum* – "out of the many one" – to form a single "United States," a single America, out of "we, the people."

XXI

How can we save our country? How do we bring men and women back together again equally while yet allowing them their differences? How do we temper the cruel and inequitable restrictions of the paternal function without losing it to the unconditional socialistic liberalism of unchecked maternity? How do we get back *all* our citizens, even those disenfranchised with our history? How do we rescue our media? How do we free our schools and our children? How do we save religion? How do we make democracy work and create a new American mythology – one where complementary opposites come together to form a "oneness," a "wholeness," from their differences, a "discriminating inclusiveness" – an American dream that is not a dream for a selected few and a nightmare for others?

The answer has been right here all along. It is inherent in the "marriage" of the paternal and maternal functions. You see, our country was founded on right and just principles. We, unfortunately, failed to carry through on our nation's promise of "justice and liberty for *all*." From the beginning, it seems, we allowed the paternal function to become a dictatorial end in itself and ignored its complementary nature, its other half, the maternal function. We didn't realize the truth. The truth is, when a patriarchal society enables its fathers to set and enforce the laws, those fathers are "guarantors" of those laws only when maternity *permits* them to be so. The paternal function has always been dependent upon the largess of maternal acceptance. If mothers do not accept the laws that fathers set, then fathers have no power, and their laws are nothing but hollow, as Hamlet so aptly put it, "words, words, words."

Allow me to use a modern mythology, and a "magical" one at that, *The Little Prince*, by Antoine de Saint-Exupery to explain. The Little Prince is from very far away, a distant asteroid we believe to be called B-612. He leaves his home in search of someone or something to help him save his tiny world and the one flowering rose on it he loves from the threat of the baobab trees that are overgrowing and overwhelming everything. Tired from his journeying, he arrives on a planet whose sole inhabitant is a royally clad King. The planet is so small, in fact, there is practically no room for anything but the king's "magnificent ermine robe." The Little Prince is awed when he discovers the King's power is not only "absolute" but also "universal," that is, the King rules over "all that," meaning the universe and all its stars. The Little Prince believes this to be true because the King wouldn't lie. The Little Prince is thrilled and, because he loves sunsets, he asks the King to order the sun to set. And here is where he learns an important lesson. The King promises he will, indeed, order the sun to set when the "conditions are favorable," about twenty minutes to eight that evening, when the sun is ready to set. You see, the King rules over everything because his "accepted authority" rests on his requiring from each subject the duty that subject can perform. If the King ordered someone to do something that person could not or does not want to do, who would be at fault, the subject or the King? The King, of course. When the Little Prince, disappointed and bored, rushes away, the King – unable to stop him – calls out, with a "magnificent air of authority," that he will make the Little Prince his ambassador.

This excerpt from that wonderful and mythological tale, *The Little Prince*, illustrates the "absolute and universal" power of paternity – when the maternal function *chooses* to obey its authority, that is! Ultimately, the paternal laws are subject to maternity's acceptance of them. And, maternity will, and should, only accept them when they are just and equitable. In this way, the circle closes on the two functions, so they are always different yet equal. The father is obeyed when mother chooses to obey him. Therefore, what went wrong in America is not the process; the process is sound. What went wrong was the unacceptable nature of the patriarchal laws, themselves. They corrupted. They became unjust and unfavorable. They discriminated against. Thus, conditions simply did not exist to allow maternity to obey them any longer. Consequently, and rightfully so, women rebelled. For, without them and their maternal function, there can be, and should be, no patriarchal law.

What all this means, in this topsy-turvy, round-about way of explaining things, is that men *can* be successful "guarantors of the law" and, thereby, carry out the paternal function *without* punishing women. The anti-feminine messages, the anti-minority messages, the anti-gay messages, are not part of the paternal function. They are cruel and unjust corruptions of that function. Men can be restrictive and discriminating without eliminating women, minorities, and the homosexual community, simply by setting "conditional" yet positive, constructive goals all members of this society can achieve and from which they can all benefit. And this is the point: We *must* set goals. We must be challenged. Fathers want us to "push the envelope," be adventurous – work hard and feel we have *earned* our rewards. While maternity fears for our safety on the backyard gym set, it is the paternal voice that urges us to swing ever higher, to brave the dangers and, thereby, overcome them – maybe. For paternity gives no guarantees. We can work hard and be "good" and still never be rewarded; in fact, we could suffer inordinately and unjustly. Consequently, it is not the end result that is important to the paternal function; it is creating and taking advantage of opportunities. These are just a few of the positive "laws" of fatherhood that we would all wish to follow. None of us would want to sacrifice them to reject the negative aspects. And we don't have to. It is only the unreasonable, corrupted paternal laws that offend the maternal function, making them impossible for maternity to accept, let alone obey. So we can have *both* the nurturing love and concern of motherhood and the conditional challenges of the father's paternal function as long as those patriarchal conditions are just and equitable and serve to build up *all* of the father's children, his sons and daughters alike.

Think again of that image of a toddler taking its first steps. With one hand it holds on to mother for comfort and support while, with the other, it reaches out to father and the promise of this new adventure, eager to get moving and gain independence. This is the America we can have, one that supports and nurtures while yet encourages us to explore and excel, to revitalize our pioneering spirit. Remember, it was our rugged individualism that made this country the greatest nation on earth. It was only when we allowed our system to disease, only when we tried to adopt different models, that we weakened. And look what has happened: Those models, which socialize the individual to the group, are now failing in the Orient and all over the world.

No, we should never have allowed our patriarchal system to become dictatorial, destructive and discriminating – and, let's be honest, it was. Yet, likewise, we should never have rejected paternity. We did both of these because we lost our mythopoeic vision. And we were wrong – in both cases. We could not see the "bigger picture." We split the screen and separated the maternal and paternal functions, misperceiving them to be opposites at antagonist odds rather than correctly perceiving them as complements of a whole, a whole best defined, not so surprisingly, as "us" – "U. S."

XXII

Before we separate, you and I, let's explore one last mythological symbol, "the Egg of Chaos." This well known Oriental image is a Taoist recognition of the male, "yang," and female, "yin," principles coming together as one. I'm certain we are all familiar with it: A circle is formed from one dark and one light hemisphere; not so ironically, each half-segment itself contains a tiny, full circle of the complementary hue. What makes this, perhaps, one of the most powerful of mythological images is that it recognizes its limits; it can only demonstrate the *tao*, that is, the "way" – it cannot ever actually reveal the mystery, for that is the nature of mysteries: they cannot be revealed – they can only hint at the "truth." And, as Pilate implored of Christ, wishing to determine if the man standing before him was truly God, "What is truth?" Indeed, that is the question. In mythological terms, the closest we can come to an answer is "truth" is the recognition that opposites are, ultimately, the same, so they must never be eliminated – one absorbed into the other – or destroyed, one by the other. Rather, their difference and equality must be embraced simultaneously. In the Egg of Chaos, the male contains the seed of the female, and the female contains the seed of the male. This means that, even though they are opposites, they each contain the other. In every opposite – male and female – is the essential presence of the other. Otherwise, they could never relate. They would be two alien structures too dissimilar to "marry" into a relationship. Therefore, men are not "from Mars," and women are not "from Venus." If they were, they could never come together as whole "earthlings." For the whole is made up of its complements which, ironically, themselves contain – each one – the entirety of the whole.

When we perceive life in this mythopoeic way – our life in contemporary America – we realize how self-destructive our former patriarchal system was and, just as importantly, how equally self-destructive our current state – our united states – of emasculation is. In short, we are our "own worst enemies." As the comic strip character Pogo once wisely quipped, "We have met the enemy, and he is us." If America falls, it will do so because its center no longer holds. The future of America is our responsibility and our destiny. We are its complements. We are the parts who create its whole while, yet, we contain its entirety. America is as much a part of each of us as we are a part of it. Will we save our country and, thereby, ourselves? Poised as we are on the verge of the 21st century, the new millennium, will we find the means to awaken our visionaries? Will we encourage them to create our mythologies, or will we march, instead, to someone else's canned slogans and "progressive" ideas? It will take all of us, men and women, to revitalize the American dream just as it will take each of us, each woman and each man, to dream a new America.

Dreams are indeed visionary. Yet what is vision? And how do we focus our vision on what is good for America? Think about it: "Vision" is a function of coordinating the viewpoints of different yet equal eyes. Consequently, what we perceive as visual "reality" is actually a "marriage" of two diverse perspectives coming together at a common focal point. You see (pardon the pun), the paradigm is here – ironically, right before our very eyes! Our "vision" for America can come about only when we can focus both perspectives – male and female – together as "one." Notice, neither is lost or sacrificed to the other. Both remain separate, equal but different, nevertheless. And the two, separate yet equal, perspectives create our vision. Now, isn't that a healing sight for sore eyes!

We began our journey by asking if we could ever win back America, the "way it used to be." Obviously, we know the answer now is a resounding "no" – never! And that's good. For we can create an America that is even better, an America where all our men and women can come together "at one," atoned – *DIFFERENT YET EQUAL.* Ironically, this is the "tao," this is the oriental "way" – but, not so ironically, as mythology predicts, opposites are ultimately revealed to be the same – "east can meet west," for it is *our* "way" too, the *AMERICAN way.* So, if we are willing, men and women together, we can rebuild America and truly make it "the home of the brave and the land of the free," as long as we realize that first we must be brave in order to earn that beloved, that cherished, freedom.

Ultimately, our goal must be to keep both "voices" alive and to never silence one or the other ever again – till death do us part.

God *and* Goddess Bless America!

WORKS CITED

Baldwin, James. *Go Tell it on the Mountain.* New York: Dell Publishing. 1953

Barthelme, Donald. *The Dead Father.* New York: Dell Publishing, 1975.

Brown, Norman O. *Life Against Death: The Psychoanalytical Meaning of History.* Middletown, Connecticut: Wesleyan University, 1959.

Clement, Catherine. *The Lives and Legends of Jacques Lacan.* Trans. Arthur Goldhammer, New York: Columbia University Press, 1983.

Chopin, Kate. *The Awakening.* In *Anthology of American Literature, Volume II,* 6th edition (683-775), General Editor, George McMichael. New Jersey: Prentice Hall, 1997.

Conroy, Pat. *The Great Santini.* New York: Avon Books, 1976

Crane, Stephen, *The Red Badge of Courage.* New York: Penguin, USA, 1976.

de Saint Exupery, Antoine. *The Little Prince.* NY: Harcourt Brace & Company, 1943.

Freud, Sigmund. "Group Psychology: Identification," vol. 18. *The Standard Edition of Complete Psychological Works of Sigmund Freud.* Trans. from the German under the general editorship of James Strachey, in collaboration with Anna Freud, assisted by Alix Strachey and Alan Tyson, 24 vols. London: Hogarth Press, 1953.

----- *Totem and Taboo,* Book V. *The Basic Writings of Sigmund Freud.* Trans. and Ed., A. A. Brill. New York: The Modern Library, 1938.

Hawthorne, Nathaniel. *The Scarlet Letter: An Authoritative Text, Background and Sources, Criticism,* edited by Sculley Bradley, et al. New York: W. W. Norton & Company, 1978.

Hemmingway, Ernest. *"The Nick Adams Stories.* New York. Simon & Schuster, 1981

Minot, Susan. "Lust," in *Fiction 100: An Anthology of Short Stories*, 7th ed. (1002-08). New Jersey: Prentice Hall, 1995.

Morris, Desmond. *The Naked Ape*, 1st American Edition. New York: McGraw-Hill, 1967.

Updike, John. *Rabbit Is Rich*. New York: Alfred A. Knopf, 1981.

Vonnegut, Kurt, Jr. *God Bless You, Mr. Rosewater: Or Pearls Before Swine*. New York: Dell, 1979.

Index